# WEALTH AND INCOME CONSEQUENCES OF EMPLOYEE OWNERSHIP

## A COMPARATIVE STUDY FROM WASHINGTON STATE

# WEALTH AND INCOME CONSEQUENCES OF EMPLOYEE OWNERSHIP

## A COMPARATIVE STUDY FROM WASHINGTON STATE

Peter A. Kardas
Adria L. Scharf
Jim Keogh

The National Center for Employee Ownership
Oakland, CA

**Wealth and Income Consequences of Employee Ownership**
By Peter A. Kardas, Adria L. Scharf, and Jim Keogh
Editing and book design by Scott S. Rodrick

First printed in the *Journal of Employee Ownership Law and Finance,* vol. 10 no. 4
(fall 1998); printed in booklet form December 1998. Reprinted September 2002.

ISBN: 0-926902-46-6

The National Center for Employee Ownership
1736 Franklin Street, 8th Floor
Oakland, CA 94612
(510) 208-1300
(510) 272-9510 (fax)
E-mail: *nceo@nceo.org*
Web site: *http://www.nceo.org/*

# Executive Summary

This study attempts to answer questions about the success of companies with employee stock ownership plans (ESOPs) in getting more wealth and income into the hands of employees. By comparing retirement assets and wages in Washington State ESOP companies with those in matched similar non-ESOP firms, the analysis shows that ESOP companies provide significantly higher retirement benefits than comparison firms. The average value (per participant) of all retirement benefits in ESOP companies (in 1995) was approximately $32,000, whereas the average value in the comparison companies was about $12,500. None of the independent variables in the analysis eliminated or significantly diminished the ESOP as an explanation for higher asset values. A large percentage of comparison companies (between 58% and 71%) had no retirement plan at all, and in those that did, employee participation rates in the plans were lower than in the ESOP companies.

Furthermore, companies with ESOPs contributed on average about 10% of pay to all retirement plans, while the comparison companies contributed on average about three percent. Whereas in those comparison companies that have retirement plans, approximately 70% of the value of the assets was in stock offered through 401(k) plans (and presumably diversified), in ESOP companies about 60% of retirement assets take the form of company stock.

The company stock held in the ESOP does not appear to come at the cost of wages. The median hourly wage of $14.72 in the ESOP firms was 8% higher than the median hourly wage in the comparison companies. At the 10th percentile of wages, hourly wages were 4% higher in the ESOP companies, while at the 90th percentile, ESOP company wages were 18% higher. Therefore, the ratio between the 90th and 10th percentiles was higher in the ESOP companies than in the comparison firms. Unions, in both ESOP and control companies, had the effect of raising wages at the 10th percentile and lowering them at the 90th, with the result that median wages for unionized control companies are significantly higher than for non-union controls. On average, the ESOP firms in this study provide a significantly higher total compensation to their employees than do their competitors, but the ratio of 90th to 10th percentile wages suggests that they do so within the framework of rewards already established in the economy.

## About the Authors

In addition to being involved in occasional research projects, Peter Kardas works with unions, workers, and businesses in Washington State on economic development, employee ownership, and worker participation projects. Adria Scharf is a doctoral student at the University of Washington, concentrating on the sociology of work. She is co-editor of *Dollars and Sense* magazine. Jim Keogh is a business retention specialist for the Washington State Department of Community, Trade, and Economic Development and managed the agency's Employee Ownership Program for nine years.

The authors thank the Ford Foundation, Richard Freeman from the National Bureau of Economic Research, and Chris Mackin of Ownership Associates for funding this research. The authors also thank Janelle Edwards and Nick Lee from the Washington State Department of Community, Trade, and Economic Development for their careful work with data input and for other assistance they provided to the project. A special thanks also to Douglas Kruse for his comments and questions on an earlier draft of the paper and for his excellent summary of the paper at the Shared Capitalism Conference in Washington, DC, May 22 and 23, 1998.

This study originally appeared in the fall 1998 issue of the *Journal of Employee Ownership Law and Finance*, published by the National Center for Employee Ownership (NCEO). For more information about this and other NCEO publications, see the back of this book.

# Introduction

In writings during the 1950s and 1960s, Louis Kelso argued that ownership by employees of company stock is necessary to create a society in which affluence is broadly shared and extremes of economic inequality reduced. If the ultimate goal of employee stock ownership is to achieve a society that has both greater equality of economic condition as well as equality of opportunity for economic gain, then it may be of interest to examine the distribution of wealth and wages in companies that have established employee stock ownership plans (ESOPs) using the tax incentives that Kelso helped inspire. Decades after the establishment of ERISA, have ESOPs lived up to their promise to share more broadly the gains of stock ownership? What are the financial benefits of ESOPs to company employees and to ESOP participants?

The study reported here begins to address these questions with data on wages and retirement plan assets in Washington State companies. We combine government wage data on ESOP companies and comparison companies with retirement plan information from a survey of those companies and from Internal Revenue Service (IRS) Form 5500 filings to estimate:

- How the value of retirement assets in ESOP companies compares to the value of retirement assets in other companies;
- How wages in ESOP companies compare to wages in comparable non-ESOP companies;
- How ESOP and control companies compare on the provision of other benefits, such as health care insurance; and
- Whether the distribution of wealth and wages is more egalitarian in the ESOP companies.

In addition, we investigate the effects of a number of independent variables, including company size, industrial sector, percentage of ownership by the ESOP, years that the plan has been in place, unionization, and company participation programs.

## Methodology and Description of Companies

### The Sample

The sample of 102 ESOP companies includes nearly every such company in Washington State that we were able to identify. We used Form 5500 data and records from the Washington State Employee Ownership Program to generate a list of all definite and potential ESOP companies in the state. We

1

then made phone calls to those companies to confirm whether they have an ESOP or a KSOP (i.e., a combined 401(k) plan and ESOP).[1]

The 499 control companies were selected by random match. For each employee stock ownership company confirmed to have an ESOP, three to seven control companies of the same employment size and industrial sector (based on the four-digit Standard Industrial Classification [SIC] code) were randomly selected from a database of all companies in the state provided by the Washington State Employment Security Department. All but three ESOP companies were matched with between three and seven controls. For three ESOP companies, there were only two possible comparison companies of the same sector available. This resulted in an average number of control companies per ESOP company of five.

Wage and employment data for 1995 for all 601 companies—102 ESOP companies and 499 matched controls—were obtained from the Employment Security Department. Wages included all gross wages[2] for employees covered by unemployment insurance.[3] Tables 1 and 2 show the distribution of companies in the wage data sample by size and industrial sector, with a column included in each table for the distribution of ESOPs nationwide. A comparison of the nationwide and Washington State data indicates that the Washington companies are fairly representative of other ESOPs in terms of size and industrial sector, except that there is a smaller percentage of companies in Washington with over 500 employees.

## The Survey

We sent surveys to all 601 companies and made follow-up phone calls to 400 of those, obtaining usable responses from 148 companies—47 companies with ESOPs and 101 comparison companies (see the appendix for a copy of the survey). Out of these usable responses, we were able to match up 37 ESOPs with 68 control companies. From survey respondents we have detailed information on the value of assets held by retirement plans, the formula by which benefit assets are allocated to employees, and the number of employees in different wage categories covered by each benefit plan. In addition, survey respondents were asked the value of salary and non-salary compensation for highly compensated employees who are not covered by unemployment insurance, whether the company is public or private, whether its employees are covered by a collective bargaining agreement, the company's age, the types of participatory management techniques used, and the degree of employee influence in various decision-making areas. For ESOP companies, the survey asked for information about the ESOP plan, including the percentage of company stock held in the ESOP trust, the percentage of payroll contributed to the plan in 1995, the basis on which stock is allocated to

**Table 1. Company Size in 1995**

| Company Size in 1995 (number of employees) | Count | | Percentage (of Sample) | | ESOPs Nationwide[a] |
|---|---|---|---|---|---|
| | ESOP | Non-ESOP | ESOP | Non-ESOP | |
| 1–49 | 38 | 244 | 37% | 49% | 34% |
| 50–99 | 16 | 101 | 16% | 20% | 19% |
| 100–199 | 23 | 58 | 23% | 12% | 16% |
| 200–299 | 3 | 26 | 3% | 5% | 14% (200–500 employees) |
| 300–399 | 5 | 13 | 5% | 3% | |
| 400+ | 9 | 21 | 9% | 4% | |
| Missing | 8 | 36 | 8% | 7% | 17% (500+ employees) |
| Total | 102 | 499 | 100% | 100% | |

[a]Data are from Prolman and Kruse (1996), appendix.

**Table 2. Industrial Sector**

| Industrial Category (SIC code) | Count | | Percentage (of sample) | | ESOPs Nationwide[a] |
|---|---|---|---|---|---|
| | ESOP | Non-ESOP | ESOP | Non-ESOP | |
| SIC1: Forestry, Fishing, Mining, Construction | 10 | 58 | 10% | 12% | 11% |
| SIC 2: Manufacturing (food, lumber, printing, chemicals) | 9 | 47 | 9% | 9% | 25% (SIC 2 & 3) |
| SIC 3: Manufacturing (metal, industrial machinery, transportation equipment) | 20 | 108 | 20% | 22% | see above |
| SIC4: Transport, Communications, Utilities | 2 | 6 | 2% | 1% | 4% |
| SIC 5: Wholesale and Retail Trade | 24 | 127 | 24% | 26% | 19% |
| SIC 6: Finance, Insurance, Real Estate | 23 | 78 | 23% | 16% | 22% |
| SIC 7: Services (taxable companies) | 7 | 40 | 7% | 8% | 18% (SIC 7 & 8) |
| SIC 8: Services (health, legal, social, engineering) | 7 | 35 | 7% | 7% | see above |
| Total | 102 | 499 | 100% | 100% | 99% |

[a]Data are from Prolman and Kruse (1996), appendix.

employee accounts, whether the plan was leveraged, and the reason(s) the ESOP was implemented.

According to survey data from ESOP companies that provided this information, the percentage of company stock owned by the ESOP trust in 1995 ranged from 0% to 100% (as summarized in table 3).[4] Of those, the ESOP owned a majority of the stock in 15 companies (39%), with four of those ESOPs owning 100% of the stock. The average percentage of ownership by the stock plans was 42% and the median was 35%. Seven ESOPs for which we had this information were publicly traded, and 35 were privately held. Four comparison companies were publicly traded, and 93 were privately held.

**Table 3.  Distribution of ESOP Companies by Percentage of Company Stock Held by ESOP Trust**

| Percentage of Stock Held by ESOP Trust | Count[a] | Percentage[b] |
|---|---|---|
| 0-24% | 13 | 33% |
| 25-49% | 11 | 28% |
| 50-74% | 8 | 21% |
| 75-100% | 7 | 18% |
| Total | 39 | 100% |

[a]Number of ESOP companies for which the percentage of ownership is known.

[b]Percentage of ESOP companies for which the percentage of ownership is known.

## IRS Form 5500

In addition to data from the survey, we procured IRS Form 5500 data[5] for tax year 1995 for 250 companies in our sample, out of which we were able to match and use 202 cases—66 ESOP companies and 136 controls. All companies that provide qualified retirement plans subject to ERISA, including ESOPs, 401(k) plans, defined benefit pension plans, and profit sharing plans, must file Form 5500 with the IRS. Companies with 100 or more participants must file Form 5500 every year. Companies with fewer than 100 participants must file Form 5500-C at least every three years; for years in which Form 5500-C is not filed, such companies must file the abbreviated version, Form 5500-R. The responses to Form 5500 identify all qualified retirement plans provided per company and give the total value of assets, net value of assets, and employer contribution for each plan. We used this data both as an accuracy check for our survey information and as a supplemental source of information.

**Table 4. Median and Mean Company Size in 1985**

| Data Source | Mean Number of Employees | | Median Number of Employees | |
| --- | --- | --- | --- | --- |
| | ESOP | Non-ESOP | ESOP | Non-ESOP |
| All companies in study | 171 | 133 | 71 | 45 |
| Matched companies that returned survey | 225 | 84 | 74 | 31 |
| Matched companies that filed 5500 forms | 194 | 185 | 85 | 65 |

Table 4 summarizes mean and median company size for all companies in the study, for ESOP and comparison companies that were both matched with each other and that returned surveys, and for ESOP and comparison companies that were matched and for which Form 5500 data was available. In general, the ESOPs had higher employment than the comparison companies, with the differences being greatest for companies that returned surveys and smallest for companies in the 5500 data. Of the 37 ESOP companies that were matched with comparison companies and for which we had survey data, there was information for 31 of them in the Form 5500 data. Of the 68 comparison companies that were matched with ESOPs and for which we had survey data, there was information for 30 in the 5500 data.

A couple of other important pieces of information about the ESOP companies and matched comparisons are: the mean number of hours worked per quarter in 1995 was 392 for the ESOP companies and 371 for the control companies. The average start date for all retirement plans in both ESOPs and controls was 1984, with a median start date of 1986 for both groups of companies. The mean start date for ESOP plans only was 1985.

## Retirement Assets

In comparing ESOPs to the matched comparison companies on benefits and income, we will examine first the value of retirement assets (including company stock), then wages, and finally the provision of other benefits. We will look at retirement assets in three ways. First, we will compare per-participant assets held in all plans in ESOP and comparison companies. Second, we will compare the percentage of payroll contributed to retirement plans by ESOP and non-ESOP companies. Finally, we will estimate the value of assets held on behalf of ESOP participants in different wage categories.

Because both ESOP and comparison companies often have more than one retirement plan (e.g., 401(k) and profit sharing plans), the task of comparing the wealth holdings of participants in the two types of companies is somewhat complex. To accurately compare employees' retirement assets in ESOP companies with retirement assets in control companies, we need a measure of benefits that pulls together the value per participant of each plan in a company. To have an accurate understanding of how ESOPs compare to typical competitors, we also must take into account the percentage of companies that do not file Form 5500.

Table 5 presents average assets per covered employee for ESOP companies and matched controls that returned surveys and for ESOPs and matched controls that filed Form 5500. The top row gives the sum of the average assets per participant for all plans listed in the third through seventh rows (401(k) plan, ESOP, etc.). This measure assumes that a participant in one plan is also a participant in every other plan, so the sum ("Sum of Average Assets per Participant") equals the total value of an individual's assets from all the different plans. But what if the participants in any one plan do not participate in any other plans? In that case, to get an average value of retirement assets per participant for the whole company, we must sum up the asset values of the various retirement plans (401(k), ESOP, etc.), then divide the result by the sum of participants for each plan. That is the value represented in the second row of the table ("Total assets of all plans ÷ sum of participants").

Both measures of assets per participant (rows 1 and 2 of table 5) indicate that ESOP companies provide substantially higher assets per participant than matched comparison companies. The differences are statistically significant, meaning that they are very unlikely to be the result of chance. (Throughout this study, when we say "significant," we refer to statistical significance, not to the magnitude of difference between the two samples.) However, the two techniques of determining assets per participant yield very different results. For companies that returned surveys, the first row seems to yield the more accurate result because the figure in the second row (for total assets divided by the sum of participants) gives us a figure for the overall average that is lower than the figure just for the ESOP plans (row 4). Use of the first measure, which assumes a participant in one plan to be a participant in all others, is given some support by tables 6 and 7, in which the participation rate in different plans (using data from the surveys) can be compared to the percentage of total employment represented by different wage categories.

Table 6, which provides retirement plan participation rates (plan participants per wage category as a percentage of total employment) for the ESOP companies, indicates that the highest overall rates are in the ESOP,

**Table 5. Assets per Participant for Several Plans, Using Survey and Form 5500 Data**

| Assets Per Participant, Different Plans | ESOP Companies, from Survey ($n = 37$) | Control Companies, from Survey (Weighted $n = 37$) | ESOP Companies, from 5500s ($n = 66$) | Control Companies, from 5500s (Weighted $n = 66$) |
|---|---|---|---|---|
| Sum of average assets per participant, all plans | $32,213* | $12,735* | $47,680*** | $24,946*** |
| Total assets of all plans ÷ sum of participants | $21,634** | $7,739** | $31,967* | $21,020*<br>$12,612[a] |
| 401(k) assets per participant | $3,796 | $8,890 | $13,021 | $14,720 |
| ESOP assets per participant | $24,260 | $0 | $20,396 | $136[b] |
| Defined benefit assets per participant | $1,254 | $410 | $3,148 | $2,203 |
| Profit sharing assets per participant | $607 | $1,464 | $10,466 | $5,013 |
| Other assets per participant | $2,295 | $1,971 | $650 | $2,873 |

*Note:* Results for the control companies are weighted so that the sum of control companies for each ESOP company equals one, thus eliminating the bias that results from there being more controls for some ESOP companies than for others. Numbers in the table represent average assets per participant for all plans for matched companies that either returned a survey or filed a Form 5500, even if the companies did not use one of the plans listed. Therefore, a zero for average assets in any plan is treated as a number and averaged together with other numbers.

[a]This number is weighted by .6 to take into account control companies that did not return the 5500 Form and to bring the number into line with survey data. See main text for more explanation.

[b]One control company reports ESOP assets on the 5500 form, though to the best of our knowledge the company did not have an ESOP trust in place in 1995.

*p < .05　　　**p < .03　　　***p < .003

401(k), and profit sharing plans, which either approach or exceed 100%.[6] The highest rates in the control companies, as indicated in table 7, are for the 401(k), defined benefit, and profit sharing plans, with rates in the 70% to 90% range. While these numbers cannot tell us that, on average, a participant in one plan is guaranteed to be a participant in all others, they do give

**Table 6. Wage Sector as Percentage of Total Employment, and Plan Participants as Percentage of Total Employment, for ESOP Companies (Data from Surveys)**

| Hourly Wage Category | Employees in Wage Category as % of Total Employment (n = 37) | ESOP Participation Rate (n = 36) | 401(k) Participation Rate (n = 10) | Defined Benefit Participation Rate (n = 2) | Profit Sharing Participation Rate (n = 2) | Other Participation Rate (n = 1) |
|---|---|---|---|---|---|---|
| Under $6 per hour | 4% | 2% | 1% | 0% | 0% | 0% |
| $6.01–$10 per hour | 23% | 11% | 11% | 1% | 3% | 0% |
| $10.01–$14 per hour | 23% | 32% | 34% | 12% | 18% | 1% |
| $14.01–$20 per hour | 23% | 29% | 55% | 37% | 75% | 11% |
| $20.01–$40 per hour | 22% | 17% | 29% | 16% | 35% | 14% |
| Over $40 per hour | 5% | 4% | 15% | 0% | 0% | 1% |
| Total | 100% | 95% | 145% | 66% | 131% | 27% |

Note: Percentages for participation rates are only for those companies that have the designated plans. Participation rates are derived by dividing the number of plan participants in each wage category by total company employment, then averaging for all ESOP companies. The n for each participation rate equals the number of companies with that kind of plan.

us some confidence that there is broad participation in most plans in ESOP companies and that the participation rate in ESOP plans is probably higher than the rate in control companies. Therefore, these figures indicate that when using the survey data, comparing the sum of assets in ESOP and control companies is a reasonable thing to do. Because participation rates appear to be lower in the control companies than in the ESOP companies— meaning that employees in the control companies are less likely to be participants in all plans—any bias will be more in the direction of inflating the control company numbers. The per-participant retirement asset calculations for ESOP companies and controls may not be accurate to the dollar, but the relationship between the values appears to be reasonable.[7]

The measure that is most accurate for the survey results may not be most accurate for the Form 5500 results, however. As we can see from row 1 of table 5, the dollar figure from the 5500 forms for the sum of assets per participant is significantly higher than the equivalent figure from the sur-

**Table 7. Wage Sector as Percentage of Total Employment and Plan Participants as Percentage of Total Employment for Control Companies (Data from Surveys)**

| Hourly Wage Category | Employees in Wage Category as % of Total Employment (n = 67) | 401(k) Participation Rate (n = 18) | Defined Benefit Participation Rate (n = 6) | Profit Sharing Participation Rate (n = 8) | Other Participation Rate (n = 1) |
|---|---|---|---|---|---|
| Under $6 per hour | 6% | 1% | 1% | 0.4% | 0% |
| $6.01–$10 per hour | 31% | 9% | 15% | 10% | 0% |
| $10.01–$14 per hour | 22% | 15% | 39% | 17% | 0% |
| $14.01–$20 per hour | 21% | 22% | 27% | 18% | 14% |
| $20.01–$40 per hour | 17% | 21% | 5% | 18% | 0% |
| Over $40 per hour | 3% | 3% | 0.4% | 11% | 9% |
| Total | 100% | 71% | 87.4% | 74.4% | 23% |

*Note:* Percentages for participation rates are only for those companies that have the designated plans. Participation rates are derived by dividing the number of plan participants in each wage category by total company employment, then averaging for all control companies. The *n* for each participation rate equals the number of companies with that kind of plan.

veys. This is true even if we look only at the 5500 results for those companies that also returned surveys. The average sum of assets per participant for surveyed ESOP companies that were matched with controls is $45,317 (*n* = 36). The discrepancy between the $45,317 (form 5500 data) and the $32,213 (from survey data) for ESOPs may be due to companies that filed the 5500 double reporting asset totals for plans that have more than one feature, e.g., a KSOP, or a profit-sharing ESOP. This assumption is supported by the other rows in Table 5. In ESOP companies, 401(k) plan assets are significantly higher in the 5500 column than in the survey column, as are profit sharing assets. For ESOP plans, the form 5500 data and the survey data are more consistent.[8]

So which numbers should we use? The survey data in row 1 of table 5 appears to accurately represent benefits for both ESOP and control companies, while the 5500 data in row 2 appears to be accurate for ESOPs but not for controls. We can, however, weight the control company responses in row 2 to take into account those comparison companies that do not have plans. Assuming that the figure for control companies should be $12,500 (close to the sum of average assets number from the survey), the weight would be approximately 0.6 ($12,500 ÷ $21,020). In all analyses in the report using 5500 data, control company responses for the second measure of assets (total of all assets divided by the sum of participants) will be weighted by 0.6.

## Interpreting the Results

The numbers in table 5 indicate that the average value of assets per participant is significantly higher in the ESOP companies than in the controls. Looking at the first two columns, representing data from the surveys, we see that the average value in the ESOP companies is $32,213, while the average value in the control companies is $12,735. The composition of the numbers differs significantly as well. For the typical ESOP participant, the ESOP represents 75% of the combined asset value of his or her retirement accounts. Of the 75% that the ESOP holds, 80% is in company stock,[9] meaning that 60% (.75 × .80) of the asset value represented by the ESOP is in company stock. Of the remaining value in the typical ESOP participant's retirement accounts, 12% is from 401(k) assets, 4% from defined benefit assets, and 2% from profit sharing plans. In the control companies, 70% of the value of the assets is from 401(k) plans, while 3% is from defined benefit plans and 11% from profit sharing plans. So while the value of the ESOP company assets is approximately $20,000 higher than the value of the control company assets, the ESOP investment is heavily concentrated in the stock of the employing company and thus carries more risk. On the other hand, the diversified piece of the ESOP participant's retirement assets (40% of 32,000) is almost identical to the total assets of non-ESOP participants.

What do these per-participant assets mean to employees at different wage levels? Looking at ESOP companies that allocate stock to employee accounts either on the basis of payroll (28 out of the 40 companies for which we have data) or payroll to a cap (another 5 companies, for a total of 33 out of 40 who responded),[10] we can calculate a number representing assets per participant per wage category.[11] The results in table 8 should be taken as suggestive only, since we are estimating what the value is of assets per employee in each company—we do not know the actual number. Furthermore, the value for the wage category between $6.01 and $10 an hour is out of line with the other wage categories, indicating that something unusual may be going on in a few companies. Also, the number for each wage category is derived from the sum of values for the various plans, and we cannot be sure that assets for the 401(k) plan, defined plans, and so on are allocated

**Table 8. Asset Values for Individuals in Different Wage Categories**

| Wage Level | Total Benefit Payment per Employee | N of Companies |
|---|---|---|
| Under $6 per hour | $6,203 | 3 |
| $6.01 to $10 per hour | $37,668 | 17 |
| $10.01 to $14 per hour | $18,220 | 23 |
| $14.01 to $20 per hour | $30,810 | 22 |
| $20.01 to $40 per hour | $62,744 | 22 |
| Over $40 per hour | $158,593 | 14 |

*Note:* Each wage category includes data only for those companies for which we were able to make calculations—i.e., zeros are treated as missing data.

by W-2. Given these caveats, the table still gives us a sense of how people at different wage brackets benefit from an average retirement asset valued at a little over $30,000.

Translated to monthly payments, if an average asset value of $32,000 earning a 5.5% interest rate is paid out monthly for 20 years, with the principal declining to zero at the end of that period, the monthly payments will equal $220.[12] If $18,200, the estimated value of retirement benefits for an employee in the $10–$14 an hour range, is paid out in the same manner, the monthly payment to the individual will be $125. The monthly value to an individual in the over-$40 per hour category would be $1,091. By contrast, 70% of the monthly income for a full-time worker in the $10–$14 per hour bracket is approximately $1,456 (before taxes). For employer-funded defined benefit pension plans, the rule has traditionally been that a covered employee could count on 70% of the last three years' salary as a retirement benefit (see Blasi and Kruse 1991, p. 94).

The average value of $32,000 is based on the current value of the assets. If the company continues to make contributions to company stock or to other retirement plans, and/or the value of the stock increases, the value of the assets will increase. It is therefore of interest to know what percentage of payroll the company is putting into retirement assets on an ongoing annual basis. The percentages in table 9 are derived by dividing a company's total compensation for 1995 (data from the Employment Security Department's database) into the amount the company reported contributing to the different plans for that year (data from the survey of companies and from Form 5500). In terms of the total contributed to all plans, the percentages are very close for both the Form 5500 and the survey data. ESOP companies in 1995 contributed between 9.6% and 10.8% of payroll to all plans, while the control companies contributed between 2.8% and 3.0% (although the percentages from the 5500 database for control companies should probably be reduced by about half because this data does not include companies that had no retirement plans). The composition of the ESOP company totals is different for the 5500 data and the survey data, with the survey data showing almost all contributions coming from contributions to the ESOP, and the 5500 data showing significant percentages for 401(k) and profit sharing plans. This difference is probably a reflection of some ESOP plans also being profit sharing and 401(k) plans. The 5500 data does not include control companies that have no plans, while the survey data does. The end result of these levels of contribution, if continued annually, would be ESOP company employees seeing the value of their retirement assets increase at three to four times the rate of comparison companies due to the increased rate of company investment alone, all other things (e.g. relative stock values) being equal.

**Table 9. Percentage of Pay Contributed to Plans**

| Percentage of Pay Contributed to: | ESOP, from Survey Data[a] (n = 37 Unless Noted) | Controls, from Survey Data (Weighted n = 37) | ESOP, from Form 5500 Data (n = 61) | Controls, from Form 5500 Data (Unweighted n = 130) |
|---|---|---|---|---|
| All plans | 10.8%* | 2.8%* | 9.6%* | 3.0%* |
| 401(k) plans | 1.0% | 1.5% | 2.5% | 1.9% |
| ESOPs | 10.0% (n = 36) | 0% | 5.6% | 0% |
| Defined benefit plans | 0% | 0.3% | 0.1% | 0.1% |
| Profit sharing plans | 0.04% | 1.0% | 1.4% | 0.7% |
| Other plans | 0.2% | 0.1% | 0% | 0.3% |

*Note:* In this table, a zero is included in the final percentage; it is not treated as missing data. Data from the 5500 forms for the control companies is unweighted because two controls and one ESOP were dropped from the calculations due to missing data or percentage of wages that appeared unreasonably high (over 200% of payroll). There were no companies that contributed between 100% and 200% of payroll to retirement plans.

[a]Numbers for the individual plans in this column do not quite add to the number for "All Plans" due to missing data for ESOP plans for one company.

*p < .01

## Independent Variable Analysis: SIC Code, Unionization, Percentage of Ownership, and Participation

For independent variable analysis we will look first at industrial sector (measured by one-digit Standard Industrial Classification code), then at unionization, percentage of ownership, and participation. Table 10 presents retirement assets by one-digit SIC code,[13] with averages both from survey data and from 5500 data. The survey shows higher asset values for ESOP companies in five out of the seven SIC codes (3 and 5–8) and lower values in SIC codes 1 and 2. The 5500 data shows higher ESOP values in all seven SIC codes. While we will explore this a bit more vigorously later when we present regression runs, it appears that SIC codes by themselves do not explain the difference in values between ESOP and control companies; i.e., the higher ESOP values are not loaded up in only a few SIC codes.

What about the independent effect of unions?[14] Table 11 presents asset per participant values just for ownership and unions as the independent variables, and table 12 looks at ownership and unionization for SIC codes 2 and 3.[15] The apparently large difference between union and nonunion control companies represented by the data from the surveys largely evapo-

**Table 10. Retirement Assets by One-Digit SIC Code**

| Assets per Participant, by 1-Digit SIC Codes | ESOP Companies | Control Companies |
|---|---|---|
| SIC Code 1 | | |
| Assets per participant, survey | $12,489 ($n = 8$)[a] | $22,148 ($n = 13$) |
| Assets per participant, 5500 | $50,852 ($n = 8$) | $15,927 ($n = 15$) |
| SIC Code 2 | | |
| Assets per participant, survey | $9,099 ($n = 5$) | $10,443 ($n = 12$) |
| Assets per participant, 5500 | $17,465 ($n = 7$) | $10,217 ($n = 12$) |
| SIC Code 3 | | |
| Assets per participant, survey | $43,389 ($n = 7$) | $23,150 ($n = 14$) |
| Assets per participant, 5500 | $30,104 ($n = 12$) | $12,634 ($n = 32$) |
| SIC Code 5 | | |
| Assets per participant, survey | $37,872 ($n = 6$) | $3,222 ($n = 12$) |
| Assets per participant, 5500 | $29,048 ($n = 15$) | $9,828 ($n = 33$) |
| SIC Code 6 | | |
| Assets per participant, survey | $87,692 ($n = 4$) | $20,807 ($n = 5$) |
| Assets per participant, 5500 | $33,963 ($n = 13$) | $14,894 ($n = 22$) |
| SIC Code 7 | | |
| Assets per participant, survey | $10,552 ($n = 4$) | $3,780 ($n = 7$) |
| Assets per participant, 5500 | $30,645 ($n = 5$) | $4,945 ($n = 8$) |
| SIC Code 8 | | |
| Assets per participant, survey | $40,844 ($n = 3$) | $15,034 ($n = 5$) |
| Assets per participant, 5500 | $31,503 ($n = 6$) | $18,719 ($n = 12$) |

*Note:* Control company numbers for 5500 data are weighted by .6 to reflect the companies that do not have retirement plans and therefore do not file Form 5500.

[a]While the *n* is 8 for both survey and 5500 data in this cell, only 6 of the companies actually overlap.

**Table 11.  Assets per Participant, Union and Nonunion Companies**

| Assets per Participant | ESOP Companies With Unions | ESOP Companies Without Unions | Control Companies With Unions | Control Companies Without Unions |
|---|---|---|---|---|
| Assets per participant, survey data | $23,612 ($n = 6$) | $33,877 ($n = 31$) | $87,498 ($n = 7$) | $6,052 ($n = 61$) |
| Assets per participant, 5500 data | $21,990 ($n = 9$) | $33,542 ($n = 57$) | $15,315 ($n = 12$) | $12,280 ($n = 122$) |

*Note:* Using survey data, the difference between union and nonunion companies, ignoring ESOP vs. control, is significant at the .001 level. The difference between ESOPs and controls for survey data is significant at the .05 level. The difference between the union and nonunion controls in the top row of this table is significant at the .0000 level. Using Form 5500 data, the difference between ESOP and controls is significant at the .0000 level.

**Table 12.  Assets per Participant for SIC Codes 2 and 3**

| Assets per Participant for: | ESOP Companies With Unions | ESOP Companies Without Unions | Control Companies With Unions | Control Companies Without Unions |
|---|---|---|---|---|
| SIC Codes 2 & 3 5500 Data | $30,274 ($n = 6$) | $23,220 ($n = 13$) | $14,758 ($n = 11$) | $11,047 ($n = 33$) |

rates in the data from the 5500 forms, though table 12 indicates that there is still a difference between union and nonunion control and ESOP companies in SIC codes 2 and 3 (though the difference is not statistically significant). According to the regression analysis summarized in table 13, the presence of an ESOP increases per participant asset value by $20,298.72 when sector, company size, and unionization are held constant. The presence of a union does not have a statistically significant effect on asset values.

What is the effect of majority ownership? The average value of assets per participant for 12 majority-owned ESOP companies is $30,694 using the survey data or $36,369 using the 5500 data, while the average value for 21 minority-owned ESOP companies is $37,000 using the survey data or (for 19 companies) $42,632 using the 5500 data. In either case the difference is around $5,600. But while the majority-owned companies appear to fare worse than those that are minority-owned, their per-person asset values are still significantly higher than the values of their matched controls, as can be seen in table 14.

**Table 13. Regression of ESOP on Asset Value, Controlling for Unionization and SIC Code**

| | Assets per Participant | |
|---|---|---|
| Variable | B | (SE) |
| ESOP (ESOP = 1) | 20298.72* | (3915.64)* |
| Unionized (1=union) | -6.16 | (4.97) |
| SIC 1 | 7730.63 | (6628.40) |
| SIC 2 | -5349.49 | (7354.37) |
| SIC 5 | -1699.03 | (5565.99) |
| SIC 6 | 3026.62 | (6017.08) |
| SIC 7 | -2412.08 | (8518.09) |
| SIC 8 | 3226.97 | (7462.38) |
| Company size | -1063.39 | (6773.68) |
| Constant | 12715.43* | (4205.78)* |
| $R^2$ | 0.15 | |
| Adjusted $R^2$ | 0.11 | |
| N | 198 | |

*$p < 0.01$

**Table 14. Asset Values for Majority and Minority-Owned Companies and Their Respective Controls**

| Asset Data from: | Majority ESOP Companies (n = 12) | Controls for Majority ESOP Companies (Weighted n = 12) | Minority ESOP Companies | Controls for Minority ESOP Companies |
|---|---|---|---|---|
| Survey data | $30,894 | $14,803 | $36,700* (n = 21) | $7,259* (weighted n = 21) |
| Form 5500 data | $35,847* | $13,978* | $42,632** (n = 19) | $10,835** (weighted n = 19) |

*$p < .01$　　**$p < .05$

It is curious why, despite the higher average values of retirement assets in the majority-owned ESOP companies compared to their matched controls, the average assets held by plans in majority-owned ESOP companies are lower in value than the average assets held by plans in minority-owned ESOPs. The expectation would be that the more stock allocated to employee accounts, the higher the value of the assets per person. Are the minority-owned companies contributing more to 401(k) or profit sharing plans than the majority-owned companies, and driving the values higher that way? The data refute this, indicating that the contribution percentages for majority- and minority-owned companies to 401(k) plans are about the same. Is there something going on at the one-digit SIC code level that could explain the difference? We cannot find anything in regression analysis. Are there fewer participants relative to total employees in the minority-owned companies, thus giving those participants more value per person? On the contrary, the ratio of participants to employees for majority-owned companies is 67%, and for minority-owned companies 89%. Does unionization have something to do with it? There is a higher percentage of unionization in the majority-owned companies, but there is no statistically significant effect of unionization on the relationship between percentage of ownership and asset value. Is there a difference in how old the plans are in the two categories of companies? There is no difference that matters. Well then, what about the fact that minority-owned companies pay better on average than the majority-owned companies? Is there a relationship between lower asset values and lower pay?

There is, in fact, a correlation of .33 between median pay and asset value ($p < .01$), but a curious thing happens when one breaks out this relationship by majority-owned and minority-owned companies. For the majority-owned companies, the correlation is .66 ($p < .01$), while for minority-owned, the correlation is –.06 (no significance). The scatterplots in figures 1 and 2 illustrate the difference.

With the majority-owned plot, it is easy to see that the asset per participant values generally increase as wages increase, but with the minority-owned companies it looks like a couple of lower-paying ESOP companies have very high asset values, which interrupts an otherwise general tendency for higher-paying companies to have higher assets. In fact, when we remove the two outliers, the correlation increases to $r = .26, p < .01$. The mean value of the assets then drops to $26,063 (Form 5500 data), nearly $10,000 below the mean value of the majority-owned companies. The correlation is still higher for the majority-owned companies (higher median pay, higher benefit levels), and there is no statistical significance in the difference between the majority and minority-owned ESOPs, so removing the two outliers does not completely clarify the relationship between percentage of ownership and asset value. But their removal does bring results more in line with expectations.

What might be the effect of participation in workplace decisions on retirement wealth? We measured participation with two sets of questions in our survey, asking companies first what employee participation tech-

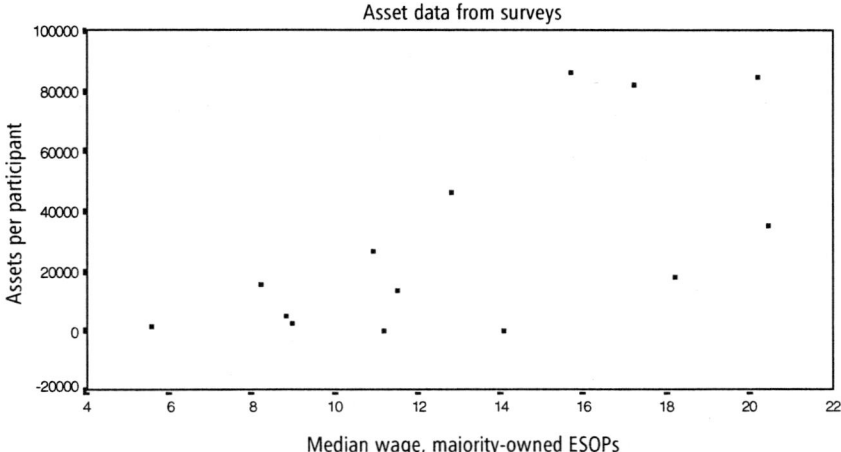

**Figure 1.  Assets by median wage, majority-owned ESOPs**

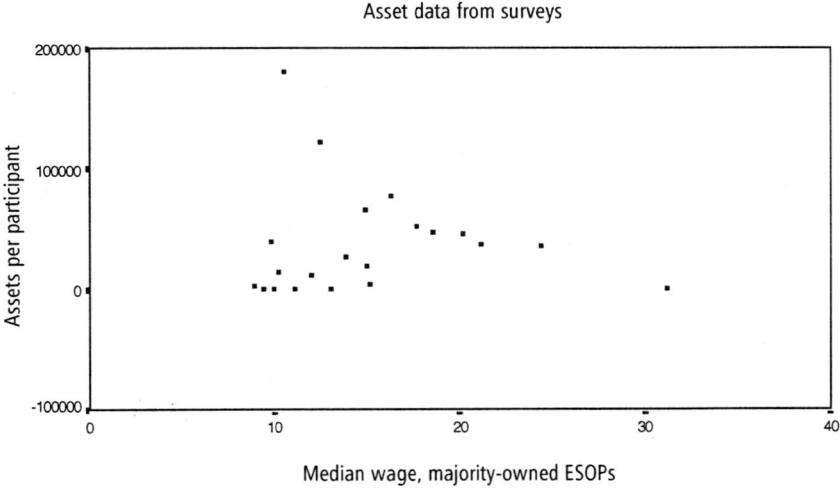

**Figure 2.  Assets by median wage, minority-owned ESOPs**

niques they use and second what degree of influence employees have over various decisions (section V of the survey in the appendix). In a 1992 study of company growth, Kardas et al. had asked companies the same question about participation techniques and found that the more techniques a company used, the more likely they were to have positive growth relative to their competitors. Keogh had found the same things in an earlier study of Washington State companies (see Keogh n.d.). The rationale for adding up techniques is that the use of a larger number of techniques can be taken as an indicator of a company's commitment to experimentation, with varied opportunities for feedback about the process, that would result in productive employee participation. Support for this theory came from the fact that majority-owned companies in the 1992 study that used more of the participative practices had higher growth rates than any other category of companies. Being participatory and majority-owned, these companies presumably would be even more likely to seek out those participation practices that both provide for employee satisfaction and lead to more productive practices.

Given our previous findings, we expected to see a similar pattern in this study: more participatory practices linked to higher growth would mean either higher wages for the employees or higher stock values that reflected the companies' success. In table 15 we can see the mean asset values from survey and 5500 data for more participatory and less participatory ESOP companies and controls, with more participation defined as the use of five or more participation techniques and less participatory the use of four or fewer. The survey data appears to indicate that more participatory ESOP companies have asset values nearly twice as large as the less participatory ESOPs (though that relationship is without statistical significance) and that both more and less participatory ESOPs have values higher than the more participatory control companies, which themselves are higher than the less participatory controls. However, this greater advantage of more participatory ESOPs disappears when we look at the 5500 data, with the less participatory ESOPs in fact having values nearly $12,000 higher than the more participatory ESOPs. Removal of one outlier from the less participatory ESOPs drops the value for that group to $28,083, less than the value for the more participatory ESOPs but not as dramatically less as with the survey data. Regression analysis confirms that, based on the 5500 data, participation has little effect on asset value when controlling for employee ownership and industrial sector. There remains a strong association, however, between employee ownership itself and asset value.[16] We get essentially the same results when using the other variable that measures employee participation by the degree of employee influence on various kinds of decisions.

What about other possible explanations for the differences in asset values between employee owned and control companies? As with the wage data, company size is negatively correlated with asset values ($-.11, p < .1$), as is the mean start date for retirement plans at the company ($-.22, p < .01$). Bigger companies or companies with earlier start dates do not have higher asset levels.[17]

**Table 15. Asset Values for ESOPs and Controls, Broken Out by Participation**

| Asset Data from: | ESOP Companies with More Participation | ESOP Companies with Less Participation | Control Companies with More Participation | Control Companies with Less Participation |
|---|---|---|---|---|
| Survey[a] | $43,981 (*n* = 18) | $23,541 (*n* = 17) | $19,306 (*n* = 26) | $13,481 (*n* = 35) |
| Form 5500[b] | $32,662 (*n* = 18) | $44,411 (*n* = 17) | $19,304 (*n* = 15) | $8,773 (*n* = 21) |

[a]Overall difference between ESOP and control companies significant at the .1 level.
[b]Overall difference between ESOP and control companies significant at the .01 level.

## Summary of Findings on Retirement Assets

Using two data sources (a survey of companies and Form 5500 records), we found asset values in ESOP companies to be roughly 2.5 times the value of assets in the matched controls. Overall, there also appeared to be higher rates of employee participation in ESOP retirement plans than in the controls, while a high percentage (between 58% and 71%) of control companies appeared to have no retirement plan at all. Within the ESOP companies, some 60% of the value of the retirement assets was in the form of company stock, while in those control companies that have retirement plans, approximately 70% of the value of the assets was in stock offered through 401(k) plans. Most ESOP companies reported allocating their stock on the basis of payroll, which meant that the value of total shares held per person varied greatly depending on a participant's wage or salary bracket. In 1995, ESOP companies contributed at least three times the percentage of payroll to retirement plans as did the control companies.

In trying to sort out the contribution made by several independent variables to the differences in asset values, we found that company categorization by one-digit SIC code did not diminish the independent explanatory power of ESOP versus non-ESOP ownership. Within ESOP companies, average asset values were lower in unionized ESOP companies than in nonunion ESOP companies. On the other hand, asset values in the unionized controls were higher than in the nonunion controls, with the greatest differences showing up in the survey data. Minority-owned ESOP companies had higher asset values than majority-owned ESOPs, though the removal of two outliers dropped the values found in minority-owned companies below the values found in majority-owned. In either case, the value of assets in majority-owned ESOP companies was significantly higher than the value of assets in the matched controls. In terms of participation, there was no clear pattern. Whereas survey data indicated that more participatory

ESOPs had much higher average asset values than less participatory ESOPs, 5500 data indicated the opposite. With both data sources, more participatory control companies had higher asset values than less participatory controls. As with wage data, company size is negatively correlated with asset values, as is the mean start date for companies' retirement plans.

## Wages

Given that the value of retirement benefits is significantly higher in ESOP companies than in comparison companies, do employees at ESOP companies typically take lower wages to make purchase of company stock possible? The simple comparison of means summarized in table 16 suggests otherwise. Here, mean and median wages, wages at the 10th and 90th percentiles, and the ratio between wages at the 90th and 10th percentiles are presented for ESOP companies and their matched controls. The results show that ESOP companies pay both higher average as well as higher median wages. The average ESOP company wage of $19.09 is 12% higher than the average control company wage of $17, and the median ESOP company wage of $14.72 is 8% higher than the median control company wage of $13.58. At the 10th percentile, wages in the ESOP companies are 4% higher than in the controls. Chance cannot be ruled out as an explanation for the differences in the mean, median, or 10th percentile wages. At the 90th percentile, ESOP wages are 18% higher than comparison wages, causing

**Table 16. Hourly Wages for ESOP and Control Companies**

| Hourly Wage | ESOP Companies | Control Companies |
|---|---|---|
| Mean hourly wage | $19.09 ($n = 90$) | $17 (weighted $n = 90$) |
| Median hourly wage | $14.72 ($n = 90$) | $13.58 (weighted $n = 90$) |
| Hourly wage at 10th percentile | $8.85 ($n = 90$) | $8.47 (weighted $n = 90$) |
| Hourly wage at 90th percentile | $30.91 ($n = 89$)* | $26.12 (weighted $n = 89$)* |
| Ratio of 90th to 10th percentile (average of all companies) | 3.49 ($n = 89$) | 3.15 ($n = 89$) |

*Note:* Results for the control companies are weighted so that the sum of control companies for each ESOP company equals one, thus eliminating the bias that results from there being more controls for some ESOP companies than for others. Companies included in the table are all but one of the ESOP companies in the Washington State Employment Security Department's database for which we have at least one match, plus, of course, the matches themselves. (One ESOP company was eliminated because it had a median hourly wage of $96, more than four times the median wage for its matched controls. Two others were removed because the companies only reported wages for the employees, not hours worked, thus making it impossible to calculate wages per hour.)

*$p < .1$

the ratio of 90th to 10th percentile wages to be 11% higher in ESOP companies.

How do these preliminary results address the equality of material condition and equality of opportunity questions raised at the beginning of the paper? Compared to their competitors, Washington State ESOP companies typically have higher pay, so employees at the middle of the pay scale are better off in terms of take-home pay working in an ESOP company than in a comparable conventional company. On the other hand, workers at the bottom of the pay scale in ESOP companies do not make much more than comparable workers in competing companies, and there is a greater distance between those at the bottom of the wage scale and those at the top than in conventional companies. There is some greater distance between the employee at the median pay level and the employee at the 90th percentile in an ESOP compared to a conventional company (2.06 versus 1.96), but the difference is not so great as the distance at the 10th percentile.[18]

What happens to these results when we control for other factors, such as industrial sector, unionization, majority ownership, company size, and workplace participation? Table 17 presents the results, for both ESOP and control companies, for the median hourly wage and hourly wages at the 10th and 90th percentiles broken out by one-digit SIC codes. While the differences vary between different SIC codes, in every case but one the median wage for the ESOP companies is higher than for the control companies. The exception is SIC code 5 (Wholesale and Retail Trade), where the ESOP median wage is nearly equal to the control company median wage. The greatest difference between ESOPs and controls is in SIC code 6 (Finance, Insurance, and Real Estate), where the difference is 15%.

It is a similar story for wages at the 90th percentile. In every case the wages in the ESOP company are higher, with the difference ranging from 8% in SIC codes 7 (Services) and 8 (Services, including legal, engineering, and educational services) to 43% in SIC code 2 (Manufacturing, including lumber, paper, printing, and petroleum refining). Wages at the 10th percentile are much closer, but again, in five out of the seven industrial sectors for which we have data, wages are higher in the ESOP companies.

What happens to these numbers when we take unionization into account? Table 18 shows median wages and wages at the 10th and 90th percentiles by ESOP and comparison companies, controlling for unionization.

The "Median wage" row in table 18 suggests that median pay in unionized control companies is 16% higher than in nonunionized controls and that median pay in unionized ESOP companies is 8% higher than in nonunion ESOPs. Furthermore, union wages for ESOP companies are 16% higher at the 10th percentile and 26% lower at the 90th percentile than are wages in nonunion ESOPs, while the equivalent percentages for the unionized

**Table 17. Median, Tenth, and Ninetieth Percentile Wages Broken Down by One-Digit SIC Code**

| Hourly Wages By One-Digit SIC Code | ESOP Companies | Control Companies |
|---|---|---|
| **SIC Code 1** | | |
| Median wage | $19.27 (*n* = 10) | $18.85 (*n* = 51) |
| Wage at 10th percentile | $11.08 (*n* = 10) | $10.56 (*n* = 50) |
| Wage at 90th percentile | $35.02 (*n* = 10) | $27.83 (*n* = 50) |
| **SIC Code 2** | | |
| Median wage | $14.62 (*n* = 9) | $12.96 (*n* = 44) |
| Wage at 10th percentile | $8.90 (*n* = 9) | $8.90 (*n* = 44) |
| Wage at 90th percentile | $39.19 (*n* = 9) | $27.35 (*n* = 43) |
| **SIC Code 3** | | |
| Median wage | $14.87 (*n* = 19) | $13.15 (*n* = 99) |
| Wage at 10th percentile | $9.37 (*n* = 19) | $8.54 (*n* = 99) |
| Wage at 90th percentile | $26.72 (*n* = 19) | $24.15 (*n* = 98) |
| **SIC code 4 (no companies in this SIC code for this analysis)** | | |
| **SIC Code 5** | | |
| Median wage | $12.41 (*n* = 21) | $12.52 (*n* = 108) |
| Wage at 10th percentile | $7.46 (*n* = 21) | $7.71 (*n* = 108) |
| Wage at 90th percentile | $25.89 (*n* = 21) | $23.50 (*n* = 106) |
| **SIC Code 6** | | |
| Median wage | $13.92 (*n* = 19) | $12.14 (*n* = 65) |
| Wage at 10th percentile | $8.23 (*n* = 19) | $7.82 (*n* = 65) |
| Wage at 90th percentile | $34.51 (*n* = 18) | $28.44 (*n* = 64) |
| **SIC Code 7** | | |
| Median wage | $12.36 (*n* = 6) | $11.59 (*n* = 27) |
| Wage at 10th percentile | $7.62 (*n* = 6) | $7.24 (*n* = 27) |
| Wage at 90th percentile | $25.91 (*n* = 6) | $23.89 (*n* = 27) |
| **SIC Code 8** | | |
| Median wage | $19.76 (*n* = 6) | $18.91 (*n* = 26) |
| Wage at 10th percentile | $11.40 (*n* = 6) | $11.86 (*n* = 26) |
| Wage at 90th percentile | $36.77 (*n* = 6) | $33.95 (*n* = 25) |

*Note:* Differences for the median wage and 10th percentile wage by SIC code are significant at the .0000 level. Differences for the 90th percentile wage by SIC code are significant at the .01 level. Since a few ESOP companies, because of the nature of their business, were matched with control companies from more than one SIC code, control companies in the above analysis are unweighted.

control companies are 30% higher (10th percentile) and 7% lower (90th percentile). These differences hold up, for the most part, when the data are broken out by one-digit SIC code. For three out of the four SIC codes (SIC codes 1 through 3) where we know union companies to be present, the wage at the 10th percentile is higher for union control companies than for non-

**Table 18. Median, 10th, and 90th Percentile Wages Broken Down by Unionization**

| Hourly Wage for: | ESOP Companies With Unions | ESOP Companies Without Unions | Control Companies With Unions | Control Companies Without Unions |
|---|---|---|---|---|
| Median wage | $15.79 | $14.57 | $15.79 | $13.62 |
| | (*n* = 11) | (*n* = 79) | (*n* = 27)* | (*n* = 393)* |
| 10th percentile wage | $10.05 | $8.69 | $10.99 | $8.45 |
| | (*n* = 11) | (*n* = 79) | (*n* = 27)** | (*n* = 392)** |
| 90th percentile wage | $23.69 | $31.93 | $24.40 | $26.11 |
| | (*n* = 11) | (*n* = 78) | (*n* = 26) | (*n* = 387) |

*$p < .1$   **$p < .01$

union controls, and in all four SIC codes the wage at the 90th percentile is lower for the union controls. For ESOP companies, the wage at the 90th percentile is lower in every case in unionized companies, while in two out of the four SIC codes, the wage at the 10th percentile is higher.

Overall, these numbers suggest that in non-ESOP companies, unions have the effect of raising the median wage as well as the wage at the 10th percentile, and that to some extent they may do the latter by holding down wages or salaries at the upper percentiles. Unions have a smaller effect in pushing up the median wage in ESOP companies, which already have a higher median wage than do the control companies. Unions in ESOP companies also appear to raise wages at the 10th percentile in some industrial sectors and to lower wages at the 90th percentile in all industrial sectors. The wage at the 90th percentile is much lower in unionized ESOP companies than in nonunion ESOP companies, while the difference between union and nonunion controls is not nearly so great. The overall median wage in unionized controls is higher than in nonunion controls due to higher wages at the 10th percentile and slightly lower wages (6% lower) at the 90th percentile. Higher wages at the 10th percentile combined with wages 26% lower at the 90th percentile would explain why the union ESOP company median wage is not higher than nonunion ESOP companies. While the numbers are only suggestive, they do conform to evidence about the effect of unions on wages presented by other researchers (see, e.g., Freeman 1994, chapter 2).

Are there other independent variables that explain some of the wage differences between ESOPs and their matched controls? Do larger companies tend to pay better than smaller firms? What about majority-owned ESOP companies and more participatory ESOP companies? Do we find the effect that we saw in the 1993 study of employment and sales growth in Washington State ESOP companies (see Kardas et al. 1994), where the combination of apparent company commitment to participation and majority ownership typically meant higher levels of growth?

One might assume that company size would be positively associated with pay (large companies have more resources, are more likely to have unions, and so on). However, the correlation between employment size and median pay is $-.1413$ ($p=.001$), with similar negative numbers for the correlation between employment size and both 10th and 90th percentile wages. This may be a reflection of the fact that some of the larger companies in the study are in retail trade and business services (temporary employment agencies, for example), which have low-paying jobs, while some of the smaller are in computer software, finance, insurance, or real estate, some of which tend to pay better. The negative relationship between employment size and pay holds up when controlling for ownership, SIC code, and unionization.

The independent effect of ownership, type of industry, and unionization can be seen in the results of a regression analysis that examines median, 10th percentile wages, and 90th percentile wages as dependent variables, and ownership, company size, industrial sector, and unionization as independent variables. As table 19 shows, statistically significant determinants of variation in median wage are the presence of an ESOP, location in sectors SIC1 and SIC 8, and unionization. Company size has an inverse relationship to median wages: smaller company size correlates with higher wages. Location in SIC 1 increases the median wage by about $5.40 compared to manufacturing work when other factors are controlled for. Location in one of the service sectors (SIC 8) similarly increases the median wage by about $5.77. The presence of an ESOP increases the median wage by $.99, and the presence of a union drives up the median wage by $1.51, controlling for other factors.

Statistically significant determinants of variation in 10th percentile wages, when controlling for other factors, are company size; location in sectors SIC1, SIC 5, and SIC 8; and unionization. Factors contributing to variation in 90th percentile wages are the presence of an ESOP; company size; location in SIC 1, SIC 2, SIC 5, SIC 6, and SIC 8. Determinants of company-level inequality as measured by the ratio of 90th to 10th percentile wages are ESOP; company size; location in sectors SIC 2, SIC 6, SIC 7, and SIC 8; and unionization.

The relationship between majority ownership and pay is more complex. On the one hand, a simple comparison of wages shows the median wage for majority-owned ESOPs to be $13.36, while the median pay of minority-owned companies is $15.07. This suggests that majority-owned ESOP companies are doing more poorly than their minority-owned cousins. On the other hand, when comparing majority-owned ESOP companies only to their matched control companies, we see that the median pay for the

**Table 19. Determinants of Median Wage, 10th and 90th Percentile, and Ratio of Wages in ESOP Companies and Comparison Companies**

| Variable | Median Wage B | (SE) | 10th Percentile B | (SE) | 90th Percentile B | (SE) | Ratio 90th/10th B | (SE) |
|---|---|---|---|---|---|---|---|---|
| ESOP | | | | | | | | |
| (ESOP = 1) | 0.99* | (0.57)* | 0.16 | (0.33) | 5.07*** | (1.81)*** | 0.40** | (0.20)** |
| Company | | | | | | | | |
| size | -0.002*** | (0.00)*** | -0.001** | (0.00)** | -0.004** | (0.00)** | 0.000* | (0.00)* |
| SIC 1 | 5.40*** | (0.77)*** | 1.86*** | (0.45)*** | 4.54* | (2.44)* | 0.05 | (0.27) |
| SIC 2 | -0.36 | (0.82) | -0.04 | (0.47) | 5.39** | (2.58)** | 0.78*** | (0.28)*** |
| SIC 5 | -0.64 | (0.63) | -0.78** | (0.36)** | -0.54 | (1.99) | 0.21 | (0.22) |
| SIC 6 | -0.83 | (0.70) | -0.61 | (0.40) | 4.52** | (2.23)** | 0.77*** | (0.24)*** |
| SIC 7 | -1.08 | (0.99) | -0.97* | (0.57)* | 0.48 | (3.09) | 0.58* | (0.34)* |
| SIC 8 | 5.77*** | (0.98)*** | 3.29*** | (0.56)*** | 9.39*** | (3.12)*** | 0.17 | (0.34) |
| Unionized | | | | | | | | |
| (1=union) | 1.51* | (0.87)* | 1.95*** | (0.50)*** | -3.85 | (2.76) | -0.87*** | (0.30)*** |
| Constant | 13.27*** | (0.47)*** | 8.52*** | (0.27)*** | 24.57*** | (1.48)*** | 2.93*** | (0.16)*** |
| $R^2$ | 0.22 | | 0.19 | | 0.07 | | 0.06 | |
| Adjusted $R^2$ | 0.20 | | 0.18 | | 0.05 | | 0.05 | |
| N | 509 | | 508 | | 501 | | 509 | |

$^*p < 0.1$      $^{**}p < 0.05$      $^{***}p < 0.01$

ESOP companies is 9% higher than pay in the controls, and pay at the 10th and 90th percentiles is higher by about the same percentage as well (see table 20). The median wage for the minority-owned ESOP companies is also higher than the wage for the matched controls (8% higher), while wages at the 10th percentile are 5% higher and at the 90th percentile 13% higher. Because wages at the 90th percentile are lower in the majority-owned com-

**Table 20. Median Wages and Wages at 90th and 10th Percentiles for Majority and Minority-Owned ESOP Companies and Their Matches**

| Wage Levels | Majority ESOP Companies ($n = 15$) | Controls for Majority ESOP Companies (Weighted $n = 15$) | Minority ESOP Companies ($n = 21$) | Controls for Minority ESOP Companies (Weighted $n = 21$) |
|---|---|---|---|---|
| Median | $13.36 | $12.30 | $15.07 | $14.01 |
| 10th percentile | $8.30 | $7.78 | $9.12 | $8.74 |
| 90th percentile | $25.15 | $23.32 | $31.39 | $27.77 |
| 90th to 10th percentile ratio | 3.03 | 3.09 | 3.41 | 3.32 |

panies, the ratio of 90th to 10th percentile wages is lower as well. While the number of companies ("n" in the table) is small and there is no statistical significance to these figures, they nevertheless suggest that majority-owned ESOP companies compare favorably to minority-owned companies in terms of wages in their own industrial sectors.

If majority-owned ESOP companies are not paying better than minority-owned companies and may even have lower wages at the upper end of the pay scale, are they more likely to pay cash dividends to employees? Not according to our evidence. Out of 32 companies that answered the question about whether employee participants received cash dividends in 1995, only one answered yes, and that company was minority-owned. They may be more likely to use dividends to pay off loans for leveraging the ESOP, but we do not know that for sure. We do know, however, that 79% of the majority-owned ESOP companies that answered the question about leveraging established their ESOP primarily with borrowed funds, as opposed to 33% of the minority-owned companies. Furthermore, the wage at the 90th percentile for the majority-owned leveraged ESOPs was $25.28, while the wage at that percentile for the majority-owned non-leveraged ESOPs was $33.23.[19] This suggests an increased debt obligation that may have an effect on pay, but the number of companies involved is too small to draw definitive conclusions about this.[20]

If percentage of ownership has little effect on wages, what about the participatory practices in a company? The result for wages, presented in table 21, indicates no discernible differences in wages for more participatory companies[21] (whether ESOP companies or controls), except that wages at the 90th percentile are quite a bit lower in the more participatory compared to the less participatory ESOP companies, though the difference is not

**Table 21.  Median, 10th, and 90th Percentile Wages Broken Down by Participation**

| Hourly Wage for: | ESOP Companies with More Participation | ESOP Companies with Less Participation | Control Companies with More Participation | Control Companies with Less Participation |
|---|---|---|---|---|
| Median Wage | $14.13 (*n* = 21) | $14.70 (*n* = 21) | $12.97 (*n* = 32) | $12.74 (*n* = 52) |
| 10th Percentile Wage | $8.66 (*n* = 21) | $9.05 (*n* = 21) | $7.88 (*n* = 32) | $8.21 (*n* = 52) |
| 90th Percentile Wage | $25.83 (*n* = 21) | $32.01 (*n* = 21) | $23.97 (*n* = 32) | $24.34 (*n* = 52) |

*Note:* The difference between ESOP and control companies was significant at the .1 level for wages at the median, 10th, and 90th percentiles.

statistically significant. Furthermore, no clear pattern with participation and wages emerges when the numbers are broken out by SIC code: higher median wages at SIC codes 2, 3, and 8 (manufacturing and certain services) for both ESOP and control participatory companies, and lower median wages at SIC codes 1, 5, and 7 (natural resource base industries and construction, FIRE, and other services). This lack of a clear pattern is borne out by regression analysis.[22]

We see basically the same results when examining the relationship between the degree of employee influence on various workplace decisions and median wages and wages at the 10th and 90th percentiles. While there is a statistically significant positive correlation between the average of the six variables measuring employee influence and wages at the 10th percentile, the significance disappears when ownership, SIC code, and unionization are entered into the equation. Bearing in mind that this variable pertains only to ESOP companies and their matches that returned surveys, the most significant explanatory variable in that equation is unionization.

One other issue concerning wages: it is reasonable to ask when reviewing this data whether the ESOP companies had higher wages than the comparison companies before the introduction of the ESOP, and in fact whether the costs associated with the ESOP might have caused companies to lower wages—even if the wages were still higher than those in the comparison companies. Reviewing wage data for 1987 and 1995 for the 20 ESOPs (and comparisons) that, based on Form 5500 data, we know introduced an ESOP after 1987 (and for which we have data in 1987 and 1995) indicates that this is not the case. The median wage for the 20 ESOP companies in 1987 (before they introduced ESOPs) was $8.66, and the median for 66 matched comparisons was $10.46. In 1995, the median wage for the ESOP companies was $12.51, and for the comparisons $13.17. For this group of companies and comparisons, therefore, the control companies had median wages 22% higher in 1987, before the introduction of the ESOP, and 5% higher in 1995 (see table 22).[23]

**Table 22. Mean and Median Wages in 1987 and 1995 for Post-1987 ESOPs and Comparison Companies**

| ESOP or control | Mean 1987 | Mean 1995 | Percentage Change | Median 1987 | Median 1995 | Percentage Change |
|---|---|---|---|---|---|---|
| ESOP | $10.18 (n = 20) | $14.96 (n = 20) | 47% | $8.66* (n = 20) | $12.51 (n = 20) | 44% |
| Control | $11.98 (n = 65) | $15.85 (n = 64) | 32% | $10.46* (n = 65) | $13.17 (n = 64) | 26% |

*p < .1

Table 23 presents the data at the 10th and 90th percentiles for the same companies. These figures suggest that the gap between 10th and 90th percentiles for this group of ESOP companies did not grow between1987 and 1995. However, the numbers must be viewed with caution because some companies introduced an ESOP in 1989 and one at least as late as 1995.

**Table 23.  1987 and 1995 Wages at the 10th and 90th Percentiles for Post-1987 ESOPs and Comparison Companies**

| ESOP or Control | 10th Percentile 1987 | 10th Percentile 1995 | Percentage Change | 90th Percentile 1987 | 90th Percentile 1995 | Percentage Change |
|---|---|---|---|---|---|---|
| ESOP | $5.29 ($n = 20$) | $7.95 ($n = 20$) | 50% | $16.21 ($n = 20$) | $23.67 ($n = 20$) | 46% |
| Control | $5.98 ($n = 66$) | $8.07 ($n = 64$) | 35% | $19.26 ($n = 61$) | $24.48 ($n = 64$) | 27% |

**Summary of Findings on Wages**

The data presented so far indicate that ESOP companies pay significantly higher wages than their matched controls, with the wages higher in all one-digit SIC code sectors. The higher wages are least apparent at the 10th percentile and most apparent at the 90th, which means that the ratio between 90th and 10th is higher in the ESOP companies than in the controls. Unions, in both ESOP and control companies, have the effect of raising wages at the 10th percentile and lowering them at the 90th, with the result that the median wage for unionized controls is significantly higher than for nonunion controls (and about the same as the median wage for both union and nonunion ESOP companies). Larger companies do not pay better than smaller companies, with the correlation in fact running slightly in the opposite direction. Both majority-owned and minority-owned ESOP companies have higher wages than their matched controls, even though the median wage for majority-owned ESOP companies is lower than the median wage for the minority-owned, due largely to the business sectors in which they compete. Participation has no consistent effect on median wages or on wages at the 10th and 90th percentiles. Finally, data from 1987 for a group of 20 ESOP companies and matched comparison companies suggest that the ESOP companies did not have higher wages than the controls before the introduction of the ESOP.

One other note about wages: while ESOP companies pay better than the matched controls, the average wage at the 25th percentile for ESOPs is $11.18, a little below the amount that a typical Washington State family of three could survive on without having to use public subsidies—if the employee were working full-time and were not living in one of the highest-cost regions of the state. This means that, on average, at least 25% of the employees in each ESOP company were below that level. Given the lower wages of $10.61 at the 25th percentile for the control companies (and the fewer number of hours worked on average per year in those companies), the percentage below the survival wage would be a bit higher in the controls. A higher wage of $13.04 at the 25th percentile at union companies (whether ESOP or not) would equal about 22% of employees at these companies being paid below the survival level.

## Supplementary Compensation Such as Stock Options

In addition to comparing ESOP and control companies on wages and retirement assets, the survey data we obtained from companies also enables us to make a comparison on stock options, cash bonuses, and the like. Table 24 lists an average dollar value per wage category for various kinds of supplementary pay. Except for the under $6 an hour category, ESOP companies on average pay more per employee than do the control companies (though the comparison is only statistically significant in the $20 to $40 an hour category). As with wages and retirement benefits, the value of these benefits to

**Table 24. Average Value of Stock Options, Overtime Pay for Exempt Employees, Cash Bonuses, and Cash Profit Sharing by Wage Category, for ESOP and Control Companies in 1995**

| Wage Category | ESOP Companies ($n = 37$) | Control Companies (Weighted $n = 37$) |
|---|---|---|
| Under $6 per hour | $0 | $57 |
| $6–$10 per hour | $420 | $46 |
| $10–$14 per hour | $262 | $200 |
| $14–$20 per hour | $1,629 | $426 |
| $20–$40 per hour | $933* | $227* |
| Over $40 per hour | $6,149 | $2,650 |

*Note:* Dollar values for each wage category are calculated by dividing the sum dollar value per wage category (data from surveys of companies) by the number of employees in that category (data from Washington State Employment Security Department). Dollar amounts represent the average for all the companies, whether or not they pay these supplementary benefits; a zero is thus counted in and is not treated as missing data.

*$p < .1$

an individual depends greatly on his or her wage category, with the average payout in the under $6 an hour category for ESOP companies equal to $0, and the average payout in the over $40 an hour category equal to $6,149.

Overall, the average per-person value for the ESOP companies is $1,688 and for the control companies $323 (n.s.). Majority-owned ESOP companies pay out less on average than do minority-owned ESOPs ($485 for 12 majority-owned companies and $2,685 for 21 minority-owned ESOP companies, which is not statistically significant). In addition, more-participatory ESOPs pay out less than do less-participatory ESOP companies ($305 for 18 more-participatory ESOPs and $3,351 for 17 less-participatory ESOP companies, which is not statistically significant). The amount of payout in different one-digit SIC codes varies as well, going from $0 for four companies in SIC code 6 (Finance, Insurance, and Real Estate), up to $5,970 in SIC code 1 (Agriculture, Forestry, Fishing, Mining, and Construction). However, regression analysis shows no statistical significance for SIC code and percentage of participation when they are included in an equation just for the ESOP companies.

What about other benefits, such as paid leave, life, accident, or disability insurance, and health benefits? Table 25 presents results taken from the survey that indicate ESOP companies are somewhat less likely to give paid leave to no employees, are much less likely to provide insurance for no employees, and are less likely to provide health benefits for no employees. The ESOP companies also appear to be less likely to provide paid leave for all, but are more likely to provide health benefits for all. None of those comparisons is statistically significant. In terms of the percentage of health benefits financed by the employer for the employee only, both ESOP and control companies finance approximately 95% of those benefits. In terms of the percentage of benefits financed by the employer for dependents, ESOP companies finance approximately 72% of those benefits, while control companies finance approximately 80%.

## Conclusion

The major findings in this study are that ESOP companies have significantly higher pay than a matched group of competitors and significantly higher values for retirement benefits as well. While most of the control group of competitors had no retirement plan at all, by definition all the ESOP companies had at least one, with the average assets in the ESOP companies valued roughly 2.5 times as high as the average assets in all control companies (including those companies that had no retirement benefits). Furthermore, as far as we can tell from the data, these retirement assets are not being financed through sacrifices in wages.

**Table 25. Provision of Paid Leave, Insurance, and Health Benefits**

| Percentages with: | ESOP Companies | Control Companies |
|---|---|---|
| Paid leave for none | 5.4% | 9.4% |
| Paid leave for some | 54.1% | 37.5% |
| Paid leave for all | 40.5% | 53.1% |
| Insurance for none | 22.9% | 43.9% |
| Insurance for some | 54.3% | 35.1% |
| Insurance for all | 22.9% | 21.1% |
| Health benefits for none | 0% | 8.3% |
| Health benefits for some | 60% | 60% |
| Health benefits for all | 40% | 31.7% |
| Health benefits wholly employer-financed | 31.4% | 34% |
| Health benefits partly employer-financed | 68.6% | 66% |

*Note:* Paid leave defined as vacations, holidays, and sick leave; $n = 37$ ESOPs, 64 controls. Insurance defined as life, accident, and/or disability insurance; $n = 35$ ESOPs, 57 controls. Health benefits defined as medical care and/or dental plans; $n = 35$ ESOPs, 53 controls.

In terms of the question we raised at the beginning about whether ESOPs contribute to greater equality of economic condition as well as to equality of economic opportunity, the answer as suggested by the study depends on one's point of view. An ESOP participant at the median wage with an average amount of assets in his or her retirement account has a bigger share of the nation's income and wealth than a comparable employee in a typical control company. On the other hand, within ESOP companies, there is a greater distance between employees at the bottom 10% of the wage scale and those in the top 10% than there is between comparable employees in the control company. In other words, there is greater inequality within the ESOP company than within the control company, though the typical (median) ESOP participant is better off than his or her typical control company counterpart. Unionization, at least in terms of wages if not in terms of asset value, diminishes the distance between the top and bottom in ESOP companies as well as in control companies.

Higher wage values at the 90th percentile (matched by higher asset values as well, at least for the large majority of companies that allocate stock on the basis of payroll) suggest that some ESOP company managers may redistribute income that otherwise would have gone to solitary or outside owners upwards rather than downwards in the organization, particularly within nonunion companies. The employee at the 50th percentile does benefit, though not as much as the employee at the 90th percentile. The employee at the 10th percentile basically does not benefit much at all, at least in terms of wages. This may be disappointing news for supporters of employee ownership who have hoped that ESOPs might set new standards for equality within the company. Rather than establishing a new direction, ESOPs appear to be operating within, perhaps even exaggerating, the framework of rewards already established in the economy.

However, this conclusion should be tempered with the understanding that ESOP companies do share ownership of the company's assets with a majority of employees through stock ownership, something that their non-ESOP competitors do not do, even if the ESOP companies do not share it with the effect of creating more equality of condition within the company. It is important to note that the total value of benefits is significantly higher in the ESOP companies than in the typical control companies; in fact, the value of the diversified assets in the comparison companies is roughly equivalent to the value of the diversified assets in the ESOP companies. Therefore, the value represented by the ESOP shares constitutes an additional benefit above the level typically provided by non-ESOP firms. In addition, the higher median wage in ESOP companies means that most ESOP participants have a greater ability to save for retirement than do their counterparts in non-ESOP comparison companies.

Nevertheless, the picture of ESOPs operating within mainstream economic and social values is reinforced by an understanding of the risk born by ESOP participants who own stock. While at one time employee stock ownership could be understood to work best as a supplementary retirement benefit (perhaps supplementary to a defined benefit pension plan), evidence from this study suggests that 60% of the value of the typical ESOP participant's retirement assets are in company stock. This means that 60% of the typical participant's retirement benefits are at risk should the company go out of business or decline dramatically in value. In most cases there is no guaranteed pension as a backup. Bearing risk in the form of stock ownership is consistent with a capitalist ethic that emphasizes risk and investment now for the sake of unguaranteed future benefits.

In terms of the possibility for ESOPs to create an alternative organizational culture, the argument has been made that it is not ownership alone that will create that culture, but the combination of ownership and participation (see Rosen and Young 1991 and Quarrey 1987). A previous study in Washington State provided evidence that more participatory, majority-owned ESOPs had higher employment and sales growth than their competitors (see Kardas et al. 1994). If we take such growth as an indicator of company strength, then we might expect that strength to show up in higher stock values. While there is some evidence for this from the survey of companies, we did not find that evidence in the Form 5500 data. Therefore, this study cannot determine whether participation increases the value of company stock, nor, for that matter, answer questions about the effect of majority ownership on stock value.

The last point raises an important issue. While the differences between ESOP companies and control companies on wages and asset values were generally sharp, expected effects of other independent variables were not always present. This may be due in part to the small number of companies in the sample for participatory and non-participatory, majority- and minority-owned, union and nonunion companies. A larger study, with more companies from more states, might be able to better tease out the effects of some of these independent variables. Such a study, if combined with interviews of employee owners and of employees in conventionally owned companies, might also be able to address questions of attitude and consciousness. How does the world look to this employee owner whose retirement assets are heavily tied up in the company where he or she works? Does it look different to union and nonunion employees? What about to employees at the bottom, middle, and top of the company's pay scale? Do the attitudes foretell a world where stock ownership helps people feel more affluent and secure and therefore in a mind to see resources more equitably shared? Or is the consciousness more symptomatic of economically anxious individuals trying to secure a future primarily through attention to their own well-being and to the well-being of their company? A study that would address the consciousness as well as the economics of employee ownership would help us better understand a phenomenon that will almost certainly grow in popularity in the years to come.

# Appendix

*Washington State Department of Community, Trade, and Economic Development*
*Washington State Employment Security Department*

## EMPLOYEE COMPENSATION AND PARTICIPATION SURVEY

The *Department of Community, Trade, and Economic Development* and the *Employment Security Department* will use the information you provide for statistical purposes and will hold the information in strict confidence. Please use your best estimates in completing the survey; precise numbers are not necessary. The survey should take approximately 15–20 minutes to fill out. **By completing the survey and mailing back to us, you will receive a comparison of your company's benefit levels to a sample of other Washington companies in your industry.** Please return the completed survey to Peter Kardas, Department of Community, Trade, and Economic Development, P.O. Box 48300, Olympia, WA 98504-8300.

Please give 1995 information if possible. If you provide information for another year, please indicate the year: _____

### Section I: Company Information

Company Name _____

Respondent's Name _____

Respondent's Title _____

Telephone number _____

This company is: Privately held _____  Publicly traded _____  Other (please specify) _____

Total company employment _____

Are any employees in this company covered by one or more collective bargaining agreements? No _____ Yes _____

If yes: Number of unionized employees _____  Name(s) of union(s) _____

How many years has your company been in business? _____

**Section II: Benefits**

*Directions:* Please answer questions about benefits your company provides its employees. Skip questions about benefits not provided by the company, or write "N/A."

Which employees at this company receive each benefit? (Check "No employees," "All employees," or as many categories of employees as are applicable.)

|  | No employees | All employees | Full Time | Part Time | Hourly | Salary | Unionized | Nonunion |
|---|---|---|---|---|---|---|---|---|
| Paid leave (i.e., vacations, holidays, sick leave) |  |  |  |  |  |  |  |  |
| Life, accident, and/or disability insurance |  |  |  |  |  |  |  |  |
| Health benefits (medical care and/or dental plans) |  |  |  |  |  |  |  |  |

Health benefits (for employees and dependents, if provided) are: Wholly employer financed _____ % for employee; _____ % for dependents
Partly employer financed _____ Percentage financed by employer: _____

Defined benefit pension (guaranteed retirement benefit), if provided, is: Wholly employer financed _____
Partly employer financed _____ Percentage financed by employer: _____

Please complete this table. This information may have been reported to the IRS on Form 5500. (Respond only for those benefits the company provides to employees.)

### RETIREMENT BENEFIT PLAN INFORMATION FOR 1995

| | Total assets at end of the 1995 plan year (Dollar Value) | Net assets (Assets minus liabilities) at end of 1995 plan year (Dollar Value) | Employer contributions to the plan in 1995 (Dollar Value) | Distributions of benefits and payments to provide benefits to participants in 1995 (Dollar Value) | Plan Year for Benefit (if not calendar year) | Benefit offered to part-time employees (yes or no)? | Minimum number of hours needed per year to receive benefits |
|---|---|---|---|---|---|---|---|
| Defined benefit pension | | | | | | | |
| 401(k) or similar savings and thrift plan | | | | | | | |
| ESOP or KSOP | | | | | | | |
| Deferred profit sharing | | | | | | | |
| Other retirement benefit: Specify ___ | | | | | | | |

What formula is used to calculate allocations of the **defined benefit pension** benefit to employee accounts? _____

Percent of payroll contributed to the **defined benefit pension** plan in 1995: _____ ; Percent of payroll allocated in 1995: _____

What is the company's matching rate for the **401(k) or savings and thrift plan?** _____

Percent of payroll contributed to the **401(k) or savings and thrift plan** in 1995: _____ ; Percent of payroll allocated: _____

On what basis is **deferred profit sharing** stock allocated to employee accounts? W-2 ____ W-2 to a cap ____ (Specify the cap:) _____

Shares distributed equally to all participants? ____ Other formula (specify) _____

Percent of payroll contributed to the **deferred profit sharing** plan in 1995: _____ ; Percent of payroll allocated: _____

About how many employees in each wage category were covered by each benefit plan? Estimate if necessary.

| | TOTAL NUMBER OF EMPLOYEES COVERED BY EACH BENEFIT PLAN IN 1995, BY WAGE CATEGORY | | | | | |
|---|---|---|---|---|---|---|
| Straight hourly wage | Under $6.00 (Under $12,000 annually) | $6.01–$10.00 (Under $20,000 annually) | $10.01–$14.00 (Under $30,000 annually) | $14.01–$20.00 (Under $42,000 annually) | $20.01–$40.00 (Under $85,000 annually) | $40.01 + |
| Defined benefit pension | | | | | | |
| 401(k) or similar savings and thrift plan | | | | | | |
| ESOP or KSOP | | | | | | |
| Deferred profit sharing | | | | | | |
| Other retirement benefit | | | | | | |
| Specify _____ | | | | | | |

What was the total value of each type of (non-wage) compensation for each wage category of employees in 1995? (If no stock options, stock bonus, premium pay, or supplemental wages were given to employees, skip this question. If you prefer, give the average amount employees in each wage category receive per year, per month, or per week, and note below the chart what you have done. Any such information about the value of non-wage compensation for different wage categories of employees would be useful.)

**ESTIMATED TOTAL VALUE OF BENEFIT COMPENSATION BY WAGE CATEGORY IN 1995 FOR EMPLOYEES COVERED BY UNEMPLOYMENT INSURANCE**
**(This may exclude some officers, owners, and highly compensated employees)**
**REPORT PART-TIME WORKERS ACCORDING TO AN HOURLY RATE**

| | Under $6.00 (Under $12,000 annually) | $6.01–$10.00 (Under $20,000 annually) | $10.01–$14.00 (Under $30,000 annually) | $14.01–$20.00 (Under $42,000 annually) | $20.01–$40.00 (Under $85,000 annually) | $40.01 + |
|---|---|---|---|---|---|---|
| Straight hourly wage | | | | | | |
| Stock options / non-ESOP stock bonus | | | | | | |
| Premium overtime pay for exempt employees | | | | | | |
| Cash bonuses / cash profit sharing / other supplemental wages | | | | | | |

If you provided the average amount employees in each wage category receive per year, month, or week, please note that here: _____

On what basis is vacation accrual provided (seniority, wages, a combination of seniority and wages _____ )?

## Section III: Compensation of Highly Compensated Employees and Owners/Officers for the Year 1995

Number of employees not covered by unemployment insurance (i.e., paid owners, officers, highly compensated employees) _____

Total salaries paid out to employees not covered by unemployment insurance _____

Total value of other forms of compensation paid to employees not covered by unemployment insurance (stock options, stock bonus plans, cash bonuses, etc.) _____

## Section IV: Employee Stock Ownership

Does this company have an employee stock ownership plan (a defined contribution plan in which this company's stock is held in a trust for employees)? _____ No _____ Yes _____ (If no, please skip the remaining questions in Section IV.)

Year the ESOP was established: _____

Percentage of company stock currently held in the ESOP trust: _____

Percentage of company stock eventually intended to be sold to the employee ownership plan: _____

Percent of payroll contributed to the plan in 1995: _____

Percent of payroll allocated in 1995: _____

Number of employees participating in the plan _____ Number of fully vested employees _____

Do employee participants receive cash dividends? No _____ Yes _____ (If yes) Total cash amount in 1995: _____

On what basis is stock allocated to employee accounts? W-2 _____ W-2 to a cap _____ (If so, what is the cap?) _____

Shares distributed equally to all participants _____ Other formula (specify) _____

What, if any, W-2 wages are excluded from the distribution formula? _____

Total value of ESOP stock held by the plan, as determined in the last valuation _____

Were there any reductions in compensation (i.e., in wages or other pension benefits) that accompanied the ESOP implementation? If yes, describe: _____

The ESOP was established in whole or in large part: With borrowed funds _____ By company contributions of stock or funds to buy stock _____ Other (explain) _____

Check the best answer(s). (You may check more than one.)

The ESOP was formed primarily:

___ as an employee benefit

___ to turn employees into owners

___ for tax advantages

___ to improve productivity

___ to purchase stock from a major owner

___ to reduce turnover

___ Other (specify) _____

___ Don't know

**Section V: Employee Participation** (If necessary, please have a human resources manager or other officer respond to the questions in this section.)

How does your company keep employees informed about the company's state of affairs?

___ Newsletter/frequent memos/E-mail/Bulletin board

___ Regular meetings

___ Other (please specify) _____

Which, if any, of the following "employee involvement" techniques does your company use?

___ Suggestion systems

___ Quality circles

___ Employee task forces

___ Autonomous work groups

___ Profit sharing

___ Participative management training

___ Labor/management training

___ Employees on Board of Directors

___ New employee orientation

___ Other (please specify)

This table measures the degree of employee influence in various workplace decisions. Please check one column for each row.

**EMPLOYEE INFLUENCE**

| Degree of Employee Influence On: | Employees have no say | Management or employer decides; employees receive information | Employee opinions are sought and considered by management | Employees decide jointly with management | Employees decide alone or mostly alone |
|---|---|---|---|---|---|
| Working conditions | | | | | |
| The way jobs are performed | | | | | |
| Pay and other compensation | | | | | |
| Hiring, firing, personnel decisions | | | | | |
| Selection of supervisors or management | | | | | |
| Company policy (e.g., investment in equipment, distribution of profits, planning) | | | | | |

**Section VI: Cooperative Ownership** (This section is to be filled out by worker cooperatives only.)

Membership share value is: fixed _____ variable _____

Are owners paid patronage dividends? No _____ Yes _____

What did it cost to become a member in 1995? _____

What is the total value of all internal capital accounts? _____

How often does the cooperative pay out to worker-members the value of those internal capital accounts? _____

## Notes

1.  Excluded from our sample of ESOP companies are a few Washington State companies that had no similar matches available due to their size or uniqueness. We also may have missed some ESOP companies that have not filed an IRS Form 5500 in several years. Note that our focus here is on ESOP companies and not companies with stock options or other forms of employee stock ownership.

2.  Included in gross wages are employee contributions to pension plans, but not company contributions. Also included are overtime pay and bonuses, but not stock options.

3.  Employees not included in the wage database are those for whom the company paid no unemployment insurance—generally, highly compensated employees, paid owners, and officers. Of the 37 ESOPs successfully matched with comparison companies, 17 said they had employees who were not covered by unemployment insurance; of those, 9 provided salary data that allowed us to calculate the average salary per uncovered employee ($119,032). For the 68 comparison companies that were matched with ESOP companies, 7 said they had officers, etc., who were not covered by unemployment insurance, and of those, 5 provided salary data that allowed for the calculation of average salary per uncovered employee ($78,922).

4.  Three ESOP companies held no stock in 1995 because the employer had not yet begun to contribute shares to the trust. In other words, the company had an ESOP, but the ESOP held no stock.

5.  The data was supplied by Larkspur Data Resources on CD-ROM, version 5.1 (Fall 1997 release) (see *http://www.larkspurdata.com*). Larkspur's data comes from the three 5500 forms that companies can file: 5500, 5500CR, and 5500X.

6.  The participation rate percentages for different wage brackets are sometimes greater than the percentage of employment represented by those brackets, which could be a function of the data used to calculate percentages of employment in each wage sector having come from the Employment Security Department while data used to determine plan participants as a percentage of total employment came both from survey data and from Employment Security Department data. This could result in a scenario in which the person who filled out the survey did not provide accurate information about wage brackets for plan participants in 1995, so that the numbers in one bracket would be higher and those in another lower, but the overall total would be accurate. On the other hand, there may really be lower participation in some wage brackets and higher numbers in others, with the higher numbers resulting from people leaving the company but remaining on the rolls as plan participants. From the data at hand, we cannot sort out the numbers more accurately than we have presented here.

7.  The higher percentage (compared to the ESOP companies) of control company employees under $10 an hour and the lower percentage over $14 an hour helps explain the lower median wage for the controls. See the discussion in the "Wages" section of the main text.

8.  The difference in dollar amounts for the comparison companies is easier to explain. Dollar figures from the 5500 forms represent only those companies that have a plan (since those without would not have to file a report), while the figures for the surveyed controls include those companies that reported having no retire-

ment plans at all. Only 29% of the matched control companies that returned surveys reported having retirement plans. Of the total population of control companies in the wage sample, 34% filed Form 5500 in 1995. Of the 125 control companies with over 100 employees, 53 filed the form, which equals a return rate of 42%. If we use the higher percentage as an indicator of the number of control company firms with retirement plans and weight 5500 responses accordingly, the sum of average assets per participant for those control companies that filed Form 5500 would be $10,477 ($24,946 × .42), which approximates the $12,735 reported on the survey.

9. The 80% figure is from Corey Rosen of the National Center for Employee Ownership, whose studies indicate that in a typical ESOP company, 20% of the value in an ESOP account is diversified out of the stock of the sponsoring company.

10. Of the other six companies that responded, one distributed shares equally to all participants, two used years of service in combination with the W-2, and three were unclear about how they allocated stock.

11. The formula was $((a/b)^* c) \div d$, where

    a = total hourly wages for a particular job category (e.g., under $6/hour)
    b = total hourly wages for all employees in the company
    c = sum of the total value of all assets
    d = mean number of participants in a particular job category (e.g., under $6/hour)

12. The average asset values of $12,500 in the comparison companies would equal a monthly payment of $88.

13. One-digit SIC, or Standard Industrial Classification, codes, as published in the Office of Management and Budget's Standard Industrial Classification Manual, are as follows: SIC code 1 is agriculture, forestry, fishing, mining, and construction; SIC codes 2 and 3 are manufacturing; SIC code 4 is transportation, communications, electric, gas, and sanitary services; SIC code 5 is wholesale and retail trade; SIC code 6 is finance, insurance, and real estate; SIC code 7 is services; SIC code 8 is services, including legal, engineering, and educational services; and SIC code 9 is public administration.

14. Data on the presence of a bargaining unit in the company came from three sources: the AFL-CIO's UNICORE database, the survey of companies that we conducted, and an earlier version of the Form 5500 database that included an indicator for the presence of a bargaining unit. It is possible that some companies that have unions did not make it into one of the databases, so the numbers should be viewed with caution.

15. The agreement with the Employment Security Department giving us access to wage data, company addresses, etc., does not allow us to present a table for all SIC codes because of the small n in certain cells. However, the effect of unionization and SIC codes is captured in the regression analysis.

16. The regression results are given in table 15a below.

17. In research conducted during the 1980s, Michael Quarrey had found a strong correlation between management philosophy and corporate performance (see Quarrey 1991). Are companies that indicate a strong management commitment to having employees become owners more likely to have higher asset values? Our survey asked for the principal reasons why a company formed an ESOP, and when

**Table 15a. Determinants of Per-Participant Assets, Controlling for Workplace Participation**

| | Assets per Participant | |
|---|---|---|
| Variable | B | (SE) |
| ESOP (ESOP = 1) | 24963.22* | (9372.61)* |
| Participation | -1211.77 | (2136.99) |
| SIC 1 | 16846.25 | (18483.31) |
| SIC 2 | -12327.35 | (15099.41) |
| SIC 5 | -10337.68 | (13857.19) |
| SIC 6 | 7343.34 | (14760.32) |
| SIC 7 | -8783.20 | (15255.21) |
| SIC 8 | -2124.91 | (16622.00) |
| Company size | -12.65 | (11.59) |
| Constant | 22141.35 | (13600.17) |
| $R^2$ | 0.18 | |
| Adjusted $R^2$ | 0.07 | |
| N | 76 | |

*$p < 0.01$

looking at data from the 5500 forms, we see a strong correlation between checking off "to turn employees into owners" and higher asset values (partial correlation of .61, when controlling for the other answers to the question, significant at the .03 level). There were no statistically significant correlations for any of the other answers. However, when looking at that question in relation to survey data, we find a slightly negative correlation with no statistical significance. So our data does not help us sort out any influence that management philosophy may have on asset values (or, more exactly, how the effect of management philosophy on company performance affects asset values).

18. Because there is a reasonable question about how typical the companies are that responded to the survey and that file 5500 reports, table 16a below shows the results for table 16 for each of those subgroups of companies. While the numbers vary somewhat from table 1 in the text (particularly in the wage differences between the ESOP and the control companies at the 10th percentile), nevertheless the basic pattern is the same. Table 16b below shows the figures for the ESOP companies and matches that returned 5500 forms in 1995 (ESOP companies are included only if there was at least one match for each company, which means that 5500 data are not reported for 14 ESOP companies for which we had data). Again, the numbers vary slightly from table 1, but the pattern is the same.

**Table 16a. Hourly Wages for ESOP and Control Companies That Responded to the Survey**

| Hourly Wage | ESOP Companies ($n = 37$) | Control Companies (Weighted $n = 37$) |
|---|---|---|
| Mean hourly wage | $18.45 | $16.25 |
| Median hourly wage | $14.91 | $13.06 |
| Hourly wage at 10th percentile | $9.00* | $8.01* |
| Hourly wage at 90th percentile | $30.04 | $25.66 |
| Ratio of 90th to 10th percentile (Average of all companies) | 3.36 | 3.30 |

*$p < .1$

**Table 16b. Hourly Wages for ESOP and Control Companies That Filed Form 5500 in 1995**

| Hourly Wage | ESOP Companies ($n = 64$) | Control Companies (Weighted $n = 64$) |
|---|---|---|
| Mean hourly wage | $19.27 | $17.08 |
| Median hourly wage | $15.14 | $14.15 |
| Hourly wage at 10th percentile | $9.28 | $8.90 |
| Hourly wage at 90th percentile | $30.15 ($n = 64$) | $26.96 |
| Ratio of 90th to 10th percentile (Average of all companies) | 3.27 | 3.09 |

19. The data for minority and majority owned, leveraged and non-leveraged ESOPs is as follows:

**Wages at the 90th Percentile for Leveraged and Unleveraged, Majority- and Minority-Owned ESOPs**

| Leveraged or Not: | Majority-Owned ESOPs | Minority-Owned ESOPs |
|---|---|---|
| Primarily Leveraged | $25.28 ($n = 11$) | $41.67 ($n = 6$) |
| Primarily Unleveraged | $33.23 ($n = 2$) | $27.96 ($n = 11$) |

20. It is also interesting that 27% of the majority-owned ESOPs are unionized (4 out of 15), as opposed to 9% of the minority-owned ESOPs (2 out of 22). Given what we saw above about the effect that unions have on wages at the 10th and 90th percentiles, this may also help explain the lower wages at the 90th percentile for majority-owned companies.

21. As in the 1992 study, less participatory firms are defined as those that use four or fewer of the listed participation approaches, and more participatory companies are defined as those that use five or more. This breaks the ESOP companies into equal groups of 21 companies. For purposes of regression analysis, we use the sum of techniques as reported by companies rather than recoding them into the two groups.

22. The regression results are as follows:

**Determinants of Median Wage, 10th and 90th Percentile, and Ratio of Wages in ESOP and Comparison Survey Respondents, Controlling for Participation**

| Variable | Median Wage | | 10th Percentile | | 90th Percentile | | Ratio 90th/10th | |
|---|---|---|---|---|---|---|---|---|
| | B | (SE) | B | (SE) | B | (SE) | B | (SE) |
| ESOP (ESOP = 1) | 1.80** | (0.78)** | 0.69 | (0.42) | 5.89** | (2.54)** | 0.36 | (0.27) |
| Participatory | -0.18 | (0.16) | -0.08 | (0.09) | -1.03* | (0.53)* | -0.10* | (0.06)* |
| Unionized (1 = union) | 1.59 | (1.13) | 1.77*** | (0.61)*** | -2.14 | (3.68) | -0.73* | (0.40)* |
| Company size | -0.002* | (0.00)* | 0.000 | (0.00) | -0.01** | (0.00)** | -0.001** | (0.00)** |
| SIC 1 | 4.16*** | (1.21)*** | 1.24* | (0.65)* | 7.05* | (3.93)* | 0.45 | (0.42) |
| SIC 2 | -2.01* | (1.28)* | -0.39 | (0.69) | -1.29 | (4.17) | 0.08 | (0.45) |
| SIC 5 | -0.93 | (1.10) | -0.49 | (0.59) | 2.00 | (3.58) | 0.30 | (0.39) |
| SIC 6 | -0.04 | (1.29) | 0.06 | (0.69) | 10.53** | (4.19)** | 1.15** | (0.45)** |
| SIC 7 | -0.41 | (1.30) | -0.33 | (0.70) | 5.21 | (4.22) | 0.84* | (0.46)* |
| SIC 8 | 5.09*** | (1.62)*** | 3.19*** | (0.87)*** | 9.62* | (5.27)* | 0.18 | (0.57) |
| Constant | 13.11*** | (1.07)*** | 8.03*** | (0.57)*** | 25.82*** | (3.47)*** | 3.27*** | (0.38)*** |
| R2 | 0.31 | | 0.26 | | 0.16 | | 0.14 | |
| Adjusted R2 | 0.25 | | 0.20 | | 0.09 | | 0.08 | |
| N | 134 | | 134 | | 134 | | 134 | |

$*p < 0.1$  $**p < 0.05$  $***p < 0.01$

23. Another possible explanation of the data is that wage levels in the soon-to-be ESOPs were growing before the introduction of the ESOP, even though they were lower than the wage levels in the comparison companies, and that post-ESOP the growth in wages continued. The work we have done to date does not enable us to evaluate the alternative explanation.

# References

Blasi, Joseph and Douglas Kruse (1991). *The New Owners*. Harper Business.

Freeman, Richard (1994). *Working Under Different Rules*. New York: Russell Sage Foundation.

Kardas, Peter, Katrina Gale, Richard Marens, Paul Sommers, and Gorm Winther (1994). "Employment and Sales Growth in Washington State Employee Ownership Companies: A Comparative Analysis." *Journal of Employee Ownership Law and Finance*, vol. 6 no. 2 (spring).

Keogh, Jim (n.d.). "A Study of Employee Ownership in Washington State." Washington State Department of Community Development.

Prolman, Susan, and Douglas Kruse (1996). "Employee Ownership Through 401(k) Plans: The NCEO–Rutgers University Study." *Journal of Employee Ownership Law and Finance*, vol. 8 no. 4 (fall) (now reprinted as chapter 2 of *Section 401(k) Plans and Employee Ownership* Oakland, CA: National Center for Employee Ownership, 1998).

Quarrey, Michael (1987). "Employee Ownership and Corporate Performance." Reprinted in Michael Quarrey and Corey Rosen, *Employee Ownership and Corporate Performance*. Oakland, CA: National Center for Employee Ownership, 1991.

Rosen, Corey, and Karen Young (1991). *Beyond Taxes: Managing an Employee Ownership Company*. Oakland, CA: National Center for Employee Ownership.

# About the NCEO and
# Its Publications

# About the NCEO

The National Center for Employee Ownership (NCEO) is widely considered to be "the single best source of information on employee ownership anywhere in the world" (*Inc.* magazine, August 2000). Established in 1981 as a nonprofit information and membership organization, it now has over 3,400 members, including companies, professionals, unions, government officials, academics, and interested individuals. It is funded entirely through the work it does.

The NCEO's mission is to provide the most objective, reliable information possible about employee ownership at the most affordable price possible. As part of the NCEO's commitment to providing objective information, it does not lobby or provide ongoing consulting services. The NCEO publishes a variety of materials explaining how employee ownership plans work, describing how companies get employee owners more involved in making decisions about their work, and reviewing the research on employee ownership. In addition, the NCEO holds dozens of seminars and conferences on employee ownership annually. These include "introduction to stock options" and "introduction to ESOPs" workshops, meetings on employee participation, international programs, and a large annual conference. The NCEO's work also includes extensive contacts with the media, both through articles written for trade and professional publications and through interviews with reporters. Finally, the NCEO has written or edited five books for commercial publishers: *The Equity Solution* (Lexington Books, 1986); *Taking Stock: Employee Ownership at Work* (Ballinger, 1986); *Employee Ownership in Public Companies* (Quantum, 1990); *Understanding Employee Ownership* (Cornell I&LR Press, 1991); and *Employee Stock Ownership Plans* (Harcourt Brace, 1996, 1999).

## NCEO Membership Benefits

NCEO members receive the following benefits:

- The bimonthly newsletter, *Employee Ownership Report.*
- Access to the members-only area of the NCEO's Web site, which includes a searchable database of over 200 members who are employee ownership consultants.
- Substantial discounts on publications and events produced by the NCEO (including this journal).
- The right to telephone or e-mail the NCEO for answers to general or specific questions regarding employee ownership.

An introductory NCEO membership costs $80 for one year ($90 outside the U.S.) and covers an entire company at all locations, or a single office of a firm offering professional services related to employee ownership and participation. Full-time students and faculty members who are not employed in the business section may join at a rate of $35 for one year ($45 outside the U.S.).

## Selected NCEO Publications

The NCEO offers a variety of publications on all aspects of employee ownership and participation, from employee stock ownership plans (ESOPs) to stock options to employee participation. Following are descriptions of some of our main publications.

We publish new books and revise old ones on a yearly basis. To obtain the most current information on what we have available, visit our extensive Web site at *www.nceo.org* or call us at 510-208-1300.

### ESOPs

- This publication, *Wealth and Income Consequences of Employee Ownership,* presents the results of a 1998 study on how employees of ESOP companies fare in relation to employees at other companies.

    Cost: $10 for NCEO members, $15 for nonmembers

- *The ESOP Reader* is an overview of the issues involved in establishing and operating an ESOP. It covers the basics of ESOP rules, feasibility, valuation, and other matters, and then discusses managing an ESOP company, including brief case studies. It is intended for publicly traded companies and anyone with a general interest in ESOPs and employee participation.

    Cost: $25 for NCEO members, $35 for nonmembers

- *Selling to an ESOP* is a guide for owners, managers, and advisors of closely held businesses. It explains how ESOPs work and then offers a comprehensive look at legal structures, valuation, financing (including self-financing), and other matters, especially the tax-deferred section 1042 "rollover" that allows owners to indefinitely defer capital gains taxation on the proceeds of the sale to the ESOP.

    Cost: $25 for NCEO members, $35 for nonmembers

- *Leveraged ESOPs and Employee Buyouts* discusses how ESOPs borrow money to buy out entire companies, purchase shares from a retiring owner, or finance new capital. Beginning with a primer on leveraged ESOPs and their uses, it then discusses contribution limits, valuation, multi-investor buyouts, legal due diligence, transaction structures, accounting, feasibility studies, financing sources, and more. It is applicable to both public and closely held companies.

Cost: $25 for NCEO members, $35 for nonmembers

- *ESOP Valuation* collects the best articles on ESOP valuation published in our journal. Topics covered include an introduction to the subject, a case study, the valuation implications of the repurchase obligation, a due diligence checklist, ESOP valuation for banks, S corporation issues, and more.

  Cost: $25 for NCEO members, $35 for nonmembers

- The *ESOP Committee Guide* describes the different types of ESOP committees, the range of goals they can address, alternative structures, member selection criteria, training, committee life cycle concerns, and other issues.

  Cost: $25 for NCEO members, $35 for nonmembers

- *How ESOP Companies Handle the Repurchase Obligation* is a short (36-page) publication that provides essays, examples, and research about the topic.

  Cost: $10 for NCEO members, $15 for nonmembers

- The *Model ESOP* contains a sample ESOP plan, with alternative provisions given to tailor the plan to individual needs. It also includes a section-by-section explanation of the plan and other supporting materials.

  Cost: $50 for NCEO members, $75 for nonmembers

- The *Employee Ownership Q&A Disk* gives Microsoft Windows users (any version from Windows 3.1 onward) point-and-click access to 500 questions and answers on all aspects of ESOPs in a fully searchable hypertext format. The keyword search allows users to search the entire file in seconds and see all the search "hits" in context. Distributed on a 1.44 MB 3.5-inch diskette with a printed manual.

  Cost: $75 for NCEO members, $100 for nonmembers

- The *ESOP Communications Sourcebook* is a looseleaf publication for ESOP companies. It includes ideas, reproducible forms, and examples on how to share financial information, explain ESOP features, and produce events to create an "ownership culture." It also addresses marketing employee ownership to customers.

Cost: $35 for NCEO members, $50 for nonmembers

- *An Introduction to ESOPs* is a 40-page booklet that explains how ESOPs work. Intended for readers who are deciding whether to implement an ESOP and also for relatively sophisticated ESOP participants who are interested in learning about the rules governing ESOPs.

    Cost: $1.75 for NCEO members, $2.50 for nonmembers; minimum order of 10 unless ordered with one of the ESOP publications listed above.

## Stock Options and Related Plans

- *The Stock Options Book* is a comprehensive resource covering the legal, tax, and design issues involved in implementing a broad-based stock option plan. Chapters cover legal rules, administrative issues, and more. It is our basic book on the subject.

    Cost: $25 for NCEO members, $35 for nonmembers

- *Stock Options: Beyond the Basics* is a more selective and advanced book than *The Stock Options Book*. Its chapters address various specialized topics such as dealing with options in a down market, preparing for an IPO, securities issues, and "evergreen" options. The appendix is a lengthy glossary of terms used in the stock plan field.

    Cost: $25 for NCEO members, $35 for nonmembers

- *Employee Stock Purchase Plans* covers how ESPPs work; tax and legal issues; administration; accounting; communicating the plan to employees; and research on what companies are doing with their plans. The book includes sample plan documents.

    Price: $25 for NCEO members, $35 for nonmembers

- *Model Equity Compensation Plans* provides examples of stock option and stock purchase plans, together with brief explanations. A diskette is included with copies of the plan documents in text and RTF formats.

    Cost: $50 for NCEO members, $75 for nonmembers

- *Current Practices in Stock Option Plan Design* is the full report on our survey of companies with broad-based stock option plans. It includes a detailed examination of plan design, use, and experience broken down by industry, size, and other categories.

Cost: $25 for NCEO members, $35 for nonmembers

- *Communicating Stock Options* offers practical ideas and information about how to explain stock options to a broad group of employees. It includes the views of experienced practitioners as well as detailed examples of how companies communicate tax consequences, financial information, and other matters to employees.

Price: $35 for NCEO members, $50 for nonmembers

- *Stock Options, Corporate Performance, and Organizational Change* presents the first serious research to examine the relationship between broadly granted stock options and company performance, and the extent of employee involvement in broad option companies.

Price: $15 for NCEO members, $25 for nonmembers

- *Equity-Based Compensation for Multinational Corporations* describes how companies can use stock options and other equity-based programs across the world to reward a global work force. It includes a country-by-country summary of tax and legal issues as well as a detailed case study.

Price: $25 for NCEO members, $35 for nonmembers

- *The Employee's Guide to Stock Options* is a book for the everyday employee that explains in an easy-to-understand format what stock is and how stock options work.

Price: $25 for both NCEO members and nonmembers

- *Incentive Compensation and Employee Ownership* takes a broad look at how companies can use incentives, ranging from stock plans to cash bonuses to gainsharing, to motivate and reward employees. It includes both technical discussions and case studies.

Price: $25 for NCEO members, $35 for nonmembers

**Other**

- *Section 401(k) Plans and Employee Ownership* focuses on how company stock is used in 401(k) plans, both in stand-alone 401(k) plans and combination 401(k)–ESOP plans ("KSOPs").

Cost: $25 for NCEO members, $35 for nonmembers

- *A Conceptual Guide to Equity-Based Compensation for Non-U.S. Companies* helps companies outside the U.S. think through how to approach employee ownership.

  Price: $25 for NCEO members, $35 for nonmembers

- *The Journal of Employee Ownership Law and Finance* is the only professional journal solely devoted to employee ownership. Articles are written by leading experts and cover ESOPs, stock options, and related subjects in depth. The *Journal* appears four times a year and usually is about 125 pages long.

  Cost for one-year subscription:
  $75 for NCEO members, $100 for nonmembers

**To join the NCEO as a member or to order the above publications, mail or fax the order form on the next page; use the secure ordering system on our Web site at *www.nceo.org* (if you visit our Web site, you can read excerpts from these publications before ordering); or telephone us at (510) 208-1300 with your credit card in hand. If you are not already a member but join at the same time you order publications, you will receive the members-only publication discounts.**

## Order Form

Complete this form and mail it with your credit card information or check to the NCEO at 1736 Franklin St., 8th Flr., Oakland, CA 94612, or fax it with your credit card information to the NCEO at 510-272-9510. If you are not already a member, you can join now to receive member discounts on the publications you order. You also can order securely online at *www.nceo.org*.

Name

Organization

Address

City, State, Zip (Country)

Telephone                    Fax                    E-mail

**Method of Payment:**  ❑ Check (payable to "NCEO")   ❑ Visa   ❑ M/C   ❑ AMEX

Credit Card Number

Signature                                        Exp. Date

*Checks are accepted only for orders from the U.S. and must be in U.S. currency.*

| Title | Qty. | Price | Total |
|---|---|---|---|
|  |  |  |  |
|  |  |  |  |
|  |  |  |  |
|  |  |  |  |

| | |
|---|---|
| Subtotal | $ |
| Sales Tax | $ |
| Shipping | $ |
| Membership | $ |
| TOTAL DUE | $ |

**Tax:** California residents add 8.25% sales tax (on publications only, not membership or subscriptions)

**Shipping:** First publication $5, each additional $1 (outside the U.S., first pub. $25, each additional $5); no shipping charges for Journal subscriptions or membership

**Introductory NCEO Membership:** $80 for one year ($90 outside the U.S.)